TED SUN

INSIDE THE
CHINESE BUSINESS MIND

TED SUN

INSIDE THE CHINESE BUSINESS MIND

A TACTICAL GUIDE FOR MANAGERS

PRAEGER

AN IMPRINT OF ABC-CLIO, LLC
Santa Barbara, California • Denver, Colorado • Oxford, England

Library of Congress Cataloging-in-Publication Data
Sun, Ted, 1972-

   Inside the Chinese business mind : a tactical guide for managers / Ted Sun.
     p. cm.
   Includes bibliographical references and index.
   ISBN 978-0-313-36519-5 (hbk. : alk. paper) — ISBN 978-0-313-36520-1 (ebook)
1. Management—China. 2. International business enterprises—China—Management.
3. Business enterprises—Social aspects—China. 4. Business etiquette—China.
5. Corporate culture—China. I. Title.
   HD70.C5S957 2010
   658.00951—dc22   2009038680

ISBN: 978-0-313-36519-5
E-ISBN: 978-0-313-36520-1

14 13 12 11 10   1 2 3 4 5

This book is also available on the World Wide Web as an eBook.
Visit www.abc-clio.com for details.

Praeger
An Imprint of ABC-CLIO, LLC

ABC-CLIO, LLC
130 Cremona Drive, P.O. Box 1911
Santa Barbara, California 93116-1911

This book is printed on acid-free paper ∞

Manufactured in the United States of America

CONTENTS

PREFACE

Over the last few decades, the shift of economic power towards China has drawn incredible attention amongst the global business community. In order to realize the incredible potential of an awakening economic power, knowledge concerning the Chinese culture calls for further education. Dozens of books on the topic and many business schools have incorporated doing business in China as part of their content. Some schools even have an entire course around the subject. Unfortunately, the majority of the materials in books and workshops continue to possess the flaws of behaviorism. They offer great entertainment, but lack the contextual understanding of how the mind learns.

In order to overcome these challenges, we conducted an International Values Study that sought to go beyond the surface-level behaviors in many books. As you will see, the findings of the study provided many fundamental shifts from conventional wisdom. Also, throughout this book, you will find fascinating "mind gems" that offer tactical insight for Western leaders based on my study and experiences of many business leaders.

CHALLENGES IN CURRENT LITERATURE

Readers wanting to tap the Chinese marketplace face two major challenges in surveying the current literature. First, they are supposed to learn an abundance of specific behaviors. Second, they are presented with a view of China as a single entity, or monolith, rather than as a country of huge diversity.

Since the Chinese culture has many unique characteristics, along with a rich history of innovation and adaptation, the monumental amount of content makes sustainable recall of such information a huge challenge. As I was doing the initial research for the book, I found dozens of books focusing on different behaviors under certain situations. In one book, each chapter provided seven to thirteen new behaviors that covered specific situations. By the end of the book, the reader was inundated by 115 behaviors they were supposed to learn and understand so they could be effective "doing business in China." Is it really possible to memorize 115 behaviors that may conflict with an entire lifetime's experiences? The situations given in these books also present a significant challenge, as many writers assume China is a country with a single culture. What the authors do not realize is that, like the United States or any European nation, significant generational, regional, and historical differences in cultures and norms exist. Furthermore, China also has drastic differences in its spoken language that add to the complexity. The challenge of behaviorism and generalization limits the amount of meaningful learning for readers, making any return on the investment of time minimal.

UNIQUENESS OF THIS BOOK

This book offers a unique approach, integrating many aspects of educational psychology into its contextual design. These will help readers recall the important aspects of Chinese business culture. After all, if you spend hours reading a book but can't remember the hundreds of behaviors discussed, was it worth your time? Rather than focusing on an abundance of behaviors, the book offers a deeper understanding of Chinese values and beliefs. Many studies have shown that values and beliefs are the foundations for thought that lead to behaviors. Like a funnel with a large area of behaviors at the top, the few values and beliefs at the bottom offer a contextual understanding of how perceptions create behaviors. This book does not pretend to give you many "cultural fish" to digest. What it offers is a solid understanding of how to fish so that you are empowered to move into the Chinese culture and be successful.

In addition to offering rich content from both a cultural and historical perspective, I decided to take an integrative approach to this book. While most books focus on the *differences* between cultures and spend abundant effort on what to do in China, the book is a synthesis of Western and Chinese cultures. The book presents the findings of the International Values Study throughout its chapters to offer profound insights about both cultures. This book doesn't just give you a lot of information on China. The material takes you through a journey of cultural exploration. It helps you build a deeper understanding of who you are within your own culture while connecting the common values and beliefs between you and the Chinese people. The book is therefore not about "When in Rome, do as the Romans do." Since knowing self is a basic Chinese virtue, the book stands on the foundation of being true to yourself while respecting another culture.

INTENDED AUDIENCE

When I first started the book, the intention was directed at helping Western business leaders achieve success in joint business ventures in China. As the journey of writing progressed, I found the writing to lead me toward an approach that would be meaningful to both Chinese and Western business leaders. Since the research behind the book investigated both Western and Chinese systems of values and beliefs, the materials offer insight for both cultures. For Western business leaders looking to conduct business in China or to further develop their understanding of self and the Chinese culture, this book will lead you towards a profound transformation in thought. Initially, the book will help you gain a better understanding of human behavior in general. As you progress through the book, you will explore your personal paradigms that define the rules of life. By being aware of these rules, your ability to understand the Chinese culture will enhance your leadership skills—developing them above and beyond the basic content of information. The book can also be an educational tool with its many Mind Gems and exercises for further exploration. Many educators can use this book from both a business and a psychological perspective, since its foundations come from both fields of study.

I also purposely and consciously use the term "leader," rather than "manager," throughout the book. Since managers are part of a positional hierarchy, leaders can be anyone who makes a conscious choice. This book offers a journey of cultural exploration for any individual who chooses to start this journey. That choice makes them a leader.

Enjoy the journey in the book; I hope you will fully engage in all of its activities so that, by the end, you will have some powerful contextual tools for understanding others with a solid foundation for self.

ACKNOWLEDGMENTS

The work represented in this book has been a fascinating journey home. I'm sure that when Jeff Olson (my editor at Praeger) asked me to consider working on this book, he had no idea how symbolic it was to me. As I went through the initial research and thought process around the enormous work in this book, I realized that there are countless applications for the ideas presented here, above and beyond the surface of doing business in China. So first of all, thank you, Jeff, for thinking of me and asking me to take on this work.

My grandfather, Tsu Chu, passed away on April 8, 2009, while I was working on the last few chapters. Aside from a sharp mind with tremendous historical wisdom, my grandpa and grandma Mary are the reasons I have the blessed life that I do. Grandpa Chu was an amazing man who came to the United States just after WWII, on a merchant marine ship. With nothing but an incredible work ethic and profound passion, he was the foundation for a proud family of three wonderful daughters. Little did I know that while raising them, he also sent money home regularly to support his family in China. He worked up to three jobs at times to ensure that his family was taken care of at a time when the world was recovering from WWII.

Grandpa was a man of precision who earned immense respect and trust while working his way up from kitchen staff to head chef at a kosher restaurant.

Grandpa was a loving father who dedicated his life to raising an educated family. He made sure each daughter completed a college degree. I guess this also rubbed off on me as well, seeing that I simply can't get enough education.

Grandpa was also a man of unconditional love. Regardless of how emotionally challenging certain situations were, Grandpa Chu always gave the support my mother needed, whether he was down the street or thousands of miles away.

Grandpa was a loving husband, who gave all that he had to his wife through 55 years of marriage. He made sure that Grandma didn't have to work in order to raise morally sound children. And when the children all graduated, Grandpa always took the time to make sure Grandma had everything she needed, no matter what.

Grandpa was a wise teacher. The one lesson that he taught me was the importance of staying in the game, whatever that game is. Through many long conversations, Grandpa Chu blessed me with lessons with a focus on long-term goals and strategic thinking at all times.

I dedicate this work to his memory—an immigrant from WWII, working from nothing to build a wonderful family with lasting impacts.

Many other key individuals played a role in the successful research foundation of the book. Special thanks go to Iris Zhu, who diligently translated the survey. The brilliant graphics design of Andrew Hippensteele created the web survey instrument to reach out into the world. David Bee, Betty Liu, Jason Liu, Marine Mao, Mariella Remund, and my Mother, Florence Sun, were instrumental in helping to gather valuable data that contributed to the foundation of this book from a research perspective. Thank you all for being part of this incredible journey.

CHAPTER 1

THE RISING STAR OF CHINA

After a full day of exploration, I lay down in bed, my mouth still tasting the delicious and unique flavors of Chinese foods I ate throughout the day, feet tingling from many miles of walking. I was exhausted. As I closed my eyes, I felt my body reject the hard mattress that was nonetheless already softened with a few blankets. A thought of having a tough time falling asleep briefly ran through my mind and disappeared as I drifted into the unconscious.

Early in the morning, between 6:45 and 7:00 A.M., my eyes opened. I was awake without any external influences; there was no alarm clock and no distinguishing noises. My mind rose with many thoughts. Thoughts about my research, about business opportunities, about my students in the coming class in Beijing, and about my work all ran through my mind. A sense of excitement filled my mind.

While this would be normal on the first few days of a trip, it repeated itself each and every day throughout my stay in Shanghai. Back in the United States, I developed a policy that allows my body to wake up naturally. My natural sleep cycle always wakes me around 9:00 or 10:00 A.M. On rare occasions, the coming excitement of the day would wake me just after 8:00 A.M. But waking before 7:00 A.M. was astonishing. Why in the world would my mind be awake on its own this early in the morning? In the first few mornings during my extended stay, I pondered the answer. After a few mornings, it came to me.

I was in Shanghai—a major city with a significant amount of international trade and growth. Something was in the air, but it was more than that. More than a mere smell or some stimulating molecules, the energy of the city waking up was drastically different. You may have experienced a situation in

◼ MIND GEM 1.1 ◼

Mind Gem 1.1: When you are visiting a foreign country like China, consider taking the time to get lost. The essence of a culture does not reside only in the common tourist areas in major cities and attractions. This essence rests in the smaller streets where the outside world remains at a distance. In those small streets, you will find the uniqueness of a culture.

Tactical steps:

1. Schedule at least 4 hours to explore an area of a city untouched by the tourist industry.
2. Check with the hotel or local police to ensure the area is relatively safe.
3. Get on a bus, subway, or taxi.
4. Upon arrival, get out and walk around for no reason other than to explore SLOWLY!
   a. See how you feel inside as you explore—consider this a confidence builder. Each new place will show you something about yourself. Both Chinese (Confucius) and Western (Socrates) philosophies begin with the exploration of self.[2,3] The external environment provides a window into yourself.

continued on page 3

which you walked into a room and felt the negative energy, knowing that someone had just had a fight in the room. Or you get a sense of danger when walking by certain dark alley. Well, it's that kind of feeling. In Shanghai, you get the sense that something great is about to happen. There is a certain vibrancy to the city.

Once I understood this sense, I made sure that my analytical mind didn't attempt to reduce it to simple reasons. A wise author once said that some things magical are meant to stay a mystery. If you analyze it too much, the magic will go away.[1] Rather than just sitting in the midst of that vibrant energy of Shanghai, I got out of bed and ventured to the streets.

Drastic Paradigm Shifts in China

China is already a major world power from an economic perspective. Countless authors and business leaders agree that it will soon be one of the dominant powers in the world, if not the most dominating power in business.[2,3] Ample economic data exists to tell the story of China's rise from its challenges of feeding its people to the prosperity it has gained over the last 45 years. What's often missing is the story behind how China arrived here and the significant transformation the country has gone through and will continue to do so. To conduct business in China successfully, understanding the fascinating history of this journey provides the foundation for effective relationships. Otherwise, you'll fall prey to what many books preach and get lost in the hundreds of behaviors you're supposed to practice in specific situations.

While the historical information may be interesting at the surface, a deeper look provides a crucial exploration and understanding of Chinese value and belief systems. Since the Chinese culture views life within the context of historical events, the past provides a foundation for many business and relational practices.[2] Throughout this book, therefore, I'll weave historical perspectives through various business concepts. The journey that many western nations took is drastically different from the one taken by China. In order to fully understand the Chinese business environment and its people, synthesizing historical context with business practices provides deeper understanding than just learning surface level behaviors.

China's Awakening

In 1964, the government set the target of modernization as the end of the 20th century.[4] That led to the policies instituted in 1979 that liberalized China's economy. Unfortunately, this was a time in which the concept of modernization was poorly understood, especially with the country's huge population needing basic necessities.

Putting this into context, imagine growing up during the 1960s and 1970s. The billions of people had a critical need for food. Children received one ration of milk per day. Since meats were scarce, each family had meat stamps that allowed them to purchase meats at local markets. Even in restaurants,

continued from page 2

b. Be conscious of what you see and how your mind attempts to translate it into your cultural assessments. The eyes of the Western mind or any culture will always be loaded with preconceived notions. Learn to separate the interpretations of what you see and the actual events occurring. In foreign countries like China, the rationale for action is drastically different than what you may think.

c. Get a sense of the people going about their daily activities.

if you ordered a meat dish, you had to pay for the food with money and meat stamps. In Shanghai, every morning meant a trip to the local market where farmers brought in their produce for sale. The better selections were only available during early morning hours. If you slept in late (like 9 A.M.), the majority of the food would be sold and little quality produce would be left. With a large majority of the population, the primary foods were rice and produce. The acquisition of fresh-caught seafood was highly prized by any family. With such scarcity, the rule of only one child per family was one method the government used to control the population growth. With billions of mouths to feed, having one child ensured a decreasing population.

During the late 1970s, China moved from "class struggle" as the basis for policies to economic development. The Chinese government focused on three principle steps to achieving modernization by the mid 21st century. The first was to eliminate the challenges of feeding and clothing their people. In order to have more than enough to feed and clothe its people, China needed to double its GDP (Gross Domestic Product) by 1980. Once the country met the basic survival needs of its people, the second step focused on doubling the GDP again by 2000. This was the milestone considered initial prosperity. So far, they've met many of these goals. The final step was the complete modernization of China.[4]

One of the largest challenges China faced was the dramatic differences in social-economic classes of people within the many regions within its borders. Along with many strategic policies in economic development, China embraced many innovative ideas from its people to achieve these ambitious goals. One may surmise that the brilliance of not having a ready blueprint for restructuring the economy provided room for innovative thought. For example, starting with the basic necessity of food, rural China used a collective farming system with a central planning movement. While this practice had existed since the late 1950s, the reform movement provided the space for some rural areas to lease the land to individual farmers instead. In a small village in the Anhui Province (East China), 18 farming families secretly divided their land with individual autonomy over each plot. In a very short time, these innovative farmers reversed the common shortage of food grains. This courageous and innovative practice earned significant respect from the local people. Within five years (by 1984), close to 99 percent of China's farming regions applied this system of individual leasing. Innovative thinking and the ability to quickly export innovative ideas throughout the country is one of the key traits that allowed China to achieve its goals.

Economic Indicators

China's massive levels of success are one of the most sustainable advancements in world economics history. From a macroeconomics level, China's Gross Domestic Product (GDP) has consistently increased more than nine percent each year for two decades. No other country has come close to such sustained growth numbers. Figure 1.1 illustrates the incredible exponential increase in China's GDP. Within 25 years of the shift to a more open economy, China became the fourth-largest trading power in the world, along with the United States, Japan, and Germany. Between 2000 and 2007, China increased foreign trade at least 20 percent. It wasn't until 2008 that China had its first drop below 20 percent. Still, it increased 17.8 percent from 2007 and brought China's foreign trade to 2.56 trillion U.S. dollars (according to General Administration of Customs).[5]

Even as the economic crisis begins to weaken many nations' GDPs, employment rates, and financial resources, China's economy continues to grow. From one perspective, China will feel the effects of this global economic crisis with a delay due to its role as a supplier of products. From another perspective, the factors that make China a dominant power continue to exist.

For example, China's level of innovation is incredible along with its ability to mass produce innovations. Throughout Chinese history, this massive level of innovation has been well documented. China's development of products

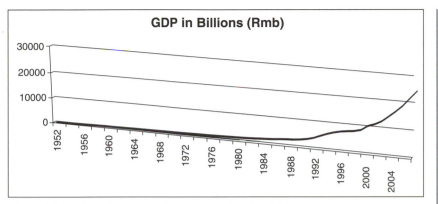

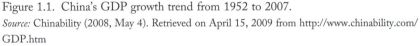

Figure 1.1. China's GDP growth trend from 1952 to 2007.
Source: Chinability (2008, May 4). Retrieved on April 15, 2009 from http://www.chinability.com/GDP.htm

such as gun powder, complex crossbows, and swords, and its ability to mass produce the innovations, were years ahead of many Western empires.

In addition to innovation in "products," China was also innovative in organizational processes and structures. For example, generals of the Han dynasty in 206 BCE had the command structures to raise and effectively command massive armies to battle in the hundreds of thousands, compared to those of the Roman empire, which consisted of 28 legions with approximately 6,000 troops total. In the late 20th century, China was able to adopt and mass produce the innovations of peasant farmers in just five years to completely transform its farming practices across the country.

The level of innovation can also be viewed from a patent perspective. While waking up to the world economies, China had established just over 1,000 patents in 2002. By 2007, China's "production" of patents rose to 5,456; that is an astonishing 38 percent increase from the previous year, when China established only 3,951 patents. During the same time period, the United States had significantly more patents (over 50,000) but only a 2.6 percent increase.[3] As more Chinese increase their awareness of the world economies and organizations like the World Intellectual Property Organization, the sustained growth in patents will surpass the annual number of patents established by the United States by 2022 (assuming a flat growth rate for both countries).

In addition to the ability to be innovative, many countries also realize the potential of consumers. As the world's most populous nation, China currently has one of the largest groups of mobile phone consumers (over 500 million) as well as a large Internet market (over 220 million).[4] Figure 1.2 illustrates the steady population growth within China. As the country relaxes its policies on the one-child law, many families are also able to afford to have more children. These two factors will influence higher population growth within the next few decades compared to the previous 50 years.

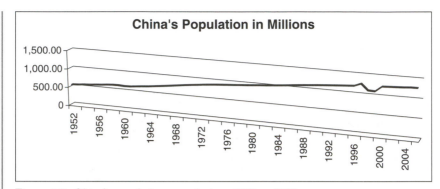

Figure 1.2. China's population growth since 1952 to 2006.
Source: Chinability (2008, May 4). Retrieved on April 15, 2009 from http://www.chinability.com/GDP.htm

GENERATIONAL GAPS

The new generation of Chinese people is technology savvy and spends more money than previous generations, which grew up struggling for food and clothes. China's population is much more diverse than the homogenous population many books theorize. While Confucian wisdom continues to guide the fundamental principles of life, the generational gaps are drastic. The generations that grew up post-World War II had many struggles with the basic necessities. Their view of the world is much more simplistic than that of later generations. For example, the older generation judges wealth by the amount of fat you have on your body. From their perspective, additional weight signaled a certain level of wealth that allowed you to purchase extra food, since the older generations didn't have the means to eat abundantly. Every time I traveled home, my grandparents' generation would tell me that I was too skinny and needed to gain some weight. From the Western perspective, I look healthy with an average body fat of 11 percent. This generation saved for a rainy day and nothing was wasted. Today, many of them continue to live with tribal behaviors of scarcity and survival. Since the retirement age is 50 or 55, almost all have retired with a modest savings. (As with the Baby Boomers, this generation represents a significant business opportunity.)

The generation that was born during the Cultural Revolution (starting in 1966) saw a traditional past emerge with many reforms in policy. Through the mid 1970s, movements to denounce any form of religion and many political maneuvers attempted to isolate China as a nation. In 1976, Premier Hua arrested the radical leaders along with their support base. This officially ended the Cultural Revolution, allowing China to focus on new strategies for feeding and clothing its people while modernizing the nation. As teenagers, this generation saw its tribal programming shattered as "blond haired" people began to show up in the streets of China. I vividly remember the mob that followed a couple of American visitors from a bus I was riding in 1980. Imagine a sight where you had only experienced people with black hair and blue coats all of your life; all of a sudden, you had people with blonde hair and very colorful clothes walking your streets. As these people walked down the streets, the mob followed them, pointed, and whispered amongst each other. This generation awoke to a shocking reality: China was now open to the Western world. While continuing to exist within the traditional values of "old" China, the new environment of Western influence opened a wide range of adaptation to different values. Some have adopted the spending mentality of Western cultures, while others held on to the saving mentality of the old. This generation represents many successful managers and executives currently in business. They are often one of the more complex generations to work with, since they embody a mixture of traditional Chinese paradigms of thinking while adapting to some of the western approaches to life and business.

The youngest generation in the workforce was born in the 1980s. Significant challenges exist in this group due to the one-child policy and the beginning of abundance. Before this period, most families still had one child with very limited basic necessities such as food and clothing. These two limitations logically fit the one-child practice. In the 1980s, while people continued the practice of having one child, the abundance of food and clothing in major cities shifted consumer behaviors. All of a sudden, parents of this generation had more than enough to provide for their family. The children of this era grew up with ample food and clothes, much like Generation Y in the United States. Unlike in the United States, many parents spoiled these children and provided a belief that there is always more. This presented a drastic shift in belief systems between the older generations, who lived in scarcity and coped with very limited resources, and the new generation, who had all that they wanted. Their upbringing shifted the spending habits towards a consumer mentality, much like in many Western countries. Rather than putting a significant portion of their income in savings, the 1980s generation spends a significant portion of their income each month. Applying the belief that there is always more, they switch jobs often, seeking a higher income to support their lifestyles. Even within the traditional family structure that rarely saw divorce as an option in the older generations, the 1980s generation is more likely to divorce when issues arise. As we will see, these three major generations have a significant influence in business practices.

REGIONAL UNIQUENESS

Categorization is a dominant practice in Western society. For the sake of census, people are grouped into large categories based on skin color or some other identifying marker. The most challenging aspect of this practice is the level of unconscious application. For example, the U.S. census has a category called "African-Americans." While the purpose of the category makes sense for statistical purposes, the application of the concept is far too vague. It ignores the many unique ethnicities inside of Africa. When I meet African-Americans, it's always fascinating to learn about the specifics of their culture and the integration with American ideologies. Rather than assuming they are one category, why not ask common questions such as: Which country in Africa are you from? What tribe or ethnic group in that country? How do they differ? One of my students at a doctoral residency program with the Swiss Management University was from Ethiopia—Deribie Mekonnen. He helped me understand that there are 85 different ethnic groups within Ethiopia. According to the Central Statistical Authority of Ethiopia, the two most populous groups are the Oromo (34.49 percent) and the Amharas (26.89 percent). While the Oromo have a belief system based on respect for nature, the Amharas are more materialistic in nature. These are two very different paradigms of thought for life. Western perspectives tend to assume that one large category defines a culture; in the case of African-Americans, the richness in the depth of each ethnic group is lost when using a simple category. The Chinese people have distinctions that are just as complex and rich.

One of the common myths, and a horrible assumption that many authors make, is the idea that China is one homogenous culture. While on the surface, 91.5 percent of the Chinese population consists of the Han ethnic group, there are 56 ethnic subgroups with histories dating back as early as 2070 BCE. Chinese also have a strong Confucius influence. Yet Taoism and Buddhism also play a critical part in the lives of many Chinese. Furthermore, the differences between generational beliefs and values are drastic. Adding into the complexity, the regional cultures are unique as well. People in Shanghai are very different from people in Beijing. For example, the conversation over meals in Beijing was dominated by national and global topics. In one lunch with ten MBA students around the table, many debated the strategic direction and actions that China should take with respect to the financial crisis in the United States. A few hundred miles away, that topic never came up in ten days of many meal conversations in Shanghai. Instead, the people spoke about fashion, the latest trends, family, and innovative ideas in business. When doing business in China, it would be a fatal mistake to assume that one practice may apply to all regions of China.

To add to the complexity, the different regions have drastically different spoken languages. While the written language is the same, there are over 300 recognized dialects in the Chinese language. Unlike the variations in most English-speaking countries, most of the dialects are different enough that one cannot understand the other. Within the United States or even in the United Kingdom, traveling an hour or two may give you a different accent in the language. An Ohioan can understand the spoken words of a Texan or a New Yorker; a Londoner can understand the spoken words of someone from Glasgow. In China, traveling just slightly outside the major city can give you a dialect that is very tough to understand. Although most of the country speaks Mandarin (the official national language), the native dialects create additional facets of cultural uniqueness.

When conducting business in China, one cannot treat China as a single culture. At the very least, China is a two-dimensional matrix with drastic generational differences on one axis and regional differences on another. In reality, the matrix is a multidimensional mix of generations, regions, educational levels, industry experiences, family structures, and individual adaptation of Western philosophies. Whether looking to start a business or market your product to China, regional and generation analyses are strategic and necessary steps.

This book will not pretend to cover all aspects of the Chinese culture nor its matrix of variations between generational and regional uniqueness. If it did, it would take years of research and thousands of pages to merely cover the complexity of the business context. Instead of focusing on content, it seeks to help you develop a process of understanding. Rather than giving you the "fish" of one specific generation in a region, the remaining chapters provide you techniques on "how to fish" in this complex business environment.

NOTES

1. Robert J. Waller, *Bridges of Madison County* (New York: Warner Books, 1992).
2. Ming-Jer Chen, *Inside Chinese Business: A Guide for Managers Worldwide* (Boston: Harvard Business Press, 2001).
3. Rebecca Fannin, *Silicon Dragon: How China Is Winning the Tech Race* (New York: McGraw-Hill, 2007), xv, xvi.
4. Mengkui Wang, *China's Economy*, translated by Bingwen Liu (Beijing, China: China International Press 2004), 4–20.
5. Xinhua News Agency, "China's foreign trade grows slowly in 2008," http://www.china.org.cn/business/news/2009-02/06/content_17238507.

CHAPTER 2

CONTEXT OVER CONTENT

We are now going to jump back into the midst of the Western world with its focus on content over context. In general, content is the "what" of a given situation; context is the environment that created or enabled a situation. One of the hidden ethical challenges in training and development is the teaching of specific behaviors (content) under certain situations. Countless organizations provide training and development for millions of people year after year. "In this situation, do this or this." Is it worthwhile? Simply ask yourself, if an ethics workshop is effective, why is there a need to come back every year? I've often found it humorous, and sad, to see some executive development professionals claiming many years of tenure in working with their clients. Such lengthy engagements show evidence of a codependent relationship. If development were successful, the individuals involved would be empowered to grow continuously without handholding from someone else. The amount of codependence that exists in many training and development practices is a considerable waste of valuable resources. The practice of teaching people behaviors in given situations creates a codependence for the individual as well. In order to learn more about new situations, more training becomes the endless and perpetual solution. This practice brings significant and sustained income for the T&D organization.

What if a fundamental principle of empowerment stood at the foundation of training and development? How might you master the context of learning to be an empowered being?

Profitability of Content

Most leaders today have very limited awareness of content and context. Having taught hundreds of leaders across the United States and in Europe, the concept of context puzzles the most successful managers and executives. This critical issue is at the core of capitalism. First, let's look at the norm of the medical system—an area in which most of you possess some personal experiences. This is one of the largest and most powerful industries built on a content focus. For most medical establishments, doctors are greatly influenced by the information they get from pharmaceutical companies. Think back to the last time you got sick and met with your doctor. What happened? You probably got some medication for your illness. If you have headaches, take aspirin (or some variation of that drug). If you have high blood pressure, here are some more pills. The regular usage of pills creates a significant source of revenue for pharmaceutical companies. The content of the problem is the illness and the treatment is often a pill. From the health perspective, many Americans are out for a quick fix addressing the surface issue (e.g., plastic surgery and a booming pharmaceutical industry).

The preparation for doing business in another country has also fallen under the disguise of a quick content fix. Reading a book about doing business in China or taking a few workshops about working with Chinese people is far from sufficient or sustainable knowledge. When looking to capitalize on the opportunities in China, behaviorist approaches are risky. The content of a situation and its appropriate behaviors are highly dependent on the other individuals' generational beliefs, regional norms, and individual experiences. Furthermore, the content approach to helping Westerners conduct business in China requires endless training workshops, resulting in high revenues for trainers.

For example, in China, one of the most significant as well as necessary events during the day is a meal. A host invites you to a meal. On the surface, you understand (thanks to a book you read) that as the honored guest, your seat is to the right of the host facing the door. Such rules are crucial to showing respect and saving face for the host and guest. What if the door is not squarely positioned or is not easily visible within the fancy décor of the restaurant? What if there is more than one guest? When a few colleagues accompany you, where should you sit? Applying basic behavior rules without understanding the context of why these rules exist could result in undesirable outcomes. In the case that you have other foreign colleagues with you, for example, the order of hierarchical positions determines the seating arrangement. In other situations, age and gender can also determine seating arrangements. This is just an example of the complexity related to where to sit. How will you react if the host asks you to select a few dishes or if the host proceeds to select dishes for you and the other guests? What is the symbolic meaning of such gestures?

While there can be an entire chapter devoted to appropriate behavior at meals, there will always be many more manifestations of situations unaccounted for in the chapter. From a scientific perspective, there are simply too many variables to predict, teach, and master appropriate behaviors. This is why focusing on understanding the context empowers you to consciously develop a set of behaviors that is consistent with the particular Chinese businessman's beliefs and values. Rather than program behaviors into your mind for specific situations, the focus on the context of understanding allows your mind to be innovative and respectful of another country's traditions.

Understanding the Context

For many business leaders, seeing and understanding the context presents significant challenges. "Content" is abundant within the norms of the Western world. In a recent workshop with leaders, it appeared that one of the common problems they faced was the lack of effective communication within the organization. The *content* in this situation is the surface issue of communication. Managers saw the economy as a reason why people weren't communicating. Yet they sent people to communication workshops who then came back with no sustainable change in behavior. It was often easy to blame specific individuals for not communicating.

As I helped these leaders see the *context* of the situation, they were astonished at the impossible request they were focusing on in content. They realized that communication between people is only a surface-level perspective. Below the noticeable behaviors, the context or the environment of a rigid hierarchical structure and top-down decision process drove people into fear of the unknown. While they preached an open-door policy, the existing context of the workplace promoted distrust and political maneuvers to get ahead. The current economic situation didn't make it any easier with the media constantly reporting layoffs around the nation. As these leaders looked at the context of their organization, they saw that it made a clear statement: "You will conform to my rules." Within this context, there was no desire for employees to communicate since the structure allowed no room for innovative thought outside the directions from top management. Seeing the context empowered leaders to realize an abundance of new ideas to address many issues, including the lack of communication.

Understanding a context is about seeing the forest from the trees. When you're not caught up in the midst of fear and authority, you get to see something much more meaningful. The meaning of communication is in "how" the message is delivered to the audience, not just the content of the message. Especially within the rich culture of China that is drastically different from that of the Western world, understanding the context of the business environment enables strategic thinking. The content is always conditional and temporary. Content changes often, based on events and people involved. The context is the relationship between people. To be successful in China, one must always be conscious of relationships, since that is the defining characteristic of an individual.[1] Context is about respect and trust in a relationship. Content is the food that you eat or the business card you receive. When Chinese businesspeople invite you to dine, the context speaks of respect. Behaviors are only surface level. The intent and values below the surface are context.

As we begin to explore the concept of context and content, one common relevant aspect of doing business in a foreign country is diversity. If you think about diversity, you might consider the content of different cultures. When thinking of the Chinese, what tends to come to mind first? For many, the recent 2008 Olympics or Chinese food may define the Chinese culture. This is a very generalized view of the Chinese. Diversity, though, resides in almost every individual. It has tremendous impact when you look at the context from within. In contextual development, the transformation of thought transcends any specific culture. For example, one could walk through a process of understanding diversity from within (e.g., how many different cultures are within you, your heritage, your family, your community; how they work together; what conflicts they have internally; your knowledge about the specific norms and values of your various cultures). Contextual development is about understanding and appreciating humanity through self-reflection. Once a leader embodies this fundamental philosophy of diversity reflection, skills for exploring new cultures develop over time. This approach to diversity is something that I have developed over many years of study. Ironically, as I studied the Chinese philosophies in preparation for authoring this book, the process for understanding self is the first step towards success, followed shortly by one's relationship with others. In Chinese philosophies, the context of trust and respect define all aspects of business, especially when dealing with foreign firms.

A "Memorable" Fish Dinner

Imagine that you are sitting at a restaurant. The waiter brings you a fish called bubba. He explains that on the fifth day of the month, everyone should have a bubba fish for luck. You take a few bites and enjoy its unique flavors, which are well outside of the norm of a salmon or sea bass. Five minutes goes by, the waiter comes with another fish. This one is called fubba by the locals. He informs you that since you are wearing the country's national colors of red and yellow, the restaurant rewards this patriotism by giving you a free fish that's favored by the locals. You welcome the gesture and thank the waiter. The arrival of fubba in your mouth has your taste buds jumping due to its rich spices. A few more bites and you're really enjoying the ethnic foods. Within a few seconds of finishing the second fish, the waiter brings you another local fish called tubba. He informs you that it's a natural custom to have tubba after fubba as it helps your foreign and unaccustomed stomach digest the bacteria naturally found on fubba. Of course, you don't want to get sick so you swallow a few large bites of the meaty fish. Feeling the weight of the fish in your stomach, you decide to have a few more drinks and relax. As the waiter serves the drink, he provides another fish called vubba. With a serious look, he lets you in on a secret. Vubba is a holy fish used only by the royalty in the old days. Eating vubba will bring you sexual prominence. You find the tale fascinating and proceed to ask—what happens if you don't eat vubba? The waiter responds with a sad look; he tells you that the royal blood no longer exists in our country. With that news, you quickly stuff a few bites of vubba into your mouth. Within a few seconds, you hear the sounds of drums in some form of celebration. The waiter expedites a nicely decorated fish called a zubba. Placing it on your table, he gives you an insistent look. By now, you are beginning to lose the enjoyment of the various native cuisines and the many stories that accompany them. And then you get the bill for the meal.

On the bill, it states a current balance of $2,345 with a perpetuating monthly fee of $236 for other fish to absorb the previous one's bacteria. Imagine that . . . a meal with a monthly addiction!

Without looking back in the text, why was fubba important? What did you really remember about the experience?

Back to Reality

Recently, I created a basic framework to better define context and content while teaching a residency for doctoral students in Vienna, Austria, at SMC University.

Managers exist and work with content. Since managers focus on performing tasks towards a specific goal and solving problems, content is what they see. Managers see a problem; they work to fix that problem. This only addresses the surface symptom, which is purely content.

Leaders exist and work with context. Since leaders focus on the people aspect of organizations, the web of relationships between people requires contextual insight. Leaders see a problem; they seek to understand the context that enabled the problem. A focus on context minimizes future occurrences of a problem.

The human mind has a mental limit on how much information it can store at one time. The typical literature on cultures is often like the fish story – full of content. It provides ample enjoyment as you are receiving the information, but very little becomes knowledge. With little responsibility for retention, your mind reaches a limit on how many fish (cultural artifacts) it can digest. The concept of serving fish to people is rather straightforward. There are always more types of fish and specific situations in which to eat them. Behaviorists use the same philosophy, preaching behaviors under specific conditions. As conditions change, the context provides a monthly source of revenue for behaviorists.

While conducting the market research for this book, a number of texts illustrated the dominance of behaviorism. In one book, the author organized thirteen chapters that made many clear distinctions on appropriate behaviors, from initial greetings to influencing decisions. While the content of the data is accurate under certain conditions, each chapter covered 7 to 13 new behaviors. By the end of the book, you had to memorize 115 new behaviors with corresponding situations. Is it realistic to regurgitate 115 behaviors in respective situations? What happens if an alternative manifestation of a situation occurred; what would be the appropriate behavior? Here lies some of the challenges in behaviorist approaches.

The approach toward understanding self and then others will be the defining context of this book. Business people need a clear understanding of the systems that drive their thinking and the respective behaviors. Going well beyond the typical behaviorist approach to doing business in China, the practical approach towards understanding the systems/processes helps you realize your ability to grow intrinsically. One of the ultimate goals of this book is to create the sustainable changes necessary for business success in China or in any country of interest. While there are dozens of books on proper behaviors, this book covers deeper concepts such as the historical influences towards complex beliefs systems and the generational differences within the United States and China. The approach seeks to create synergy from understanding the roots of two unique cultures.

NOTE

1. Ming-Jer Chen, *Inside Chinese Business: A Guide for Managers Worldwide* (Boston: Harvard Business Press, 2001).

2.1

GOING BEYOND
BEHAVIORISM

Before moving on to tell you all about the wonderful aspects of Chinese culture and how to thrive in that business environment, it's important that you know where you come from and stand. It is the start of any journey. Like a GPS navigation system, you have to know the current location before you can plot your path strategically to the destination. Two major concerns will always trip up a Western business leader: practicing behaviors without realizing the historical and philosophical context, and judging events and people based on one's Western programming (e.g., what is ethical in developed countries?).

The world of Western business thrives in behaviorism. John Watson (1878–1958) and B. F. Skinner (1904–1990) were the founding fathers of behaviorism. Within this school of thought, inputs (stimulus) and responding behaviors (response) are the primary focus of study. But think—are human beings so simplistic as to repeat a response to a certain stimulus?

As in the previous fish story, your response to the different types of fish was unique based on the symbolism behind the fish, the previous context of your experiences, the pressures from the waiter, the voice of your stomach, and your mental agreement. Within any given situation, the people involved are unique. You are in a unique mental framework with unique experiences building up to that moment. The situations are unique as well as the environment of the moment. Each of these factors has a multiplicity of perspectives to complicate the situational context. Blindly applying a behavior, assuming you remember it from a workshop or book, can cause significant unexpected drama. Worse yet, the lack of understanding may further diminish business relationships. The historical and theoretical understanding of the given situational context, including its participants, calls for going well beyond behaviorist approaches.

Recently, I taught a leadership course in an MBA program in China. Thirty-five managers and executives from a wide variety of organizational backgrounds, from government to business, filled the room. Before arriving in class, I received a recommendation from a colleague concerning the way to teach the class. He said, "When you teach in China, the students expect their professors to impart wisdom. So you have to spend a lot of time preparing lectures." I pondered the concept for a minute and saw the behaviorist approach. This being my first time teaching a Chinese student body, conventional wisdom might call for compliance to those who have experienced the Chinese classroom full of business executives and managers. Some might even call it foolish to stick with my method of teaching (andragogical and constructivism). Ask yourself, what would you do in such a situation? Comply with recommendations from experienced individuals with certain levels of outcomes, or create your own approach for unknown outcomes? Extending yourself to China may call for many similar decisions. Comply, adopt, or innovate—which approach will you take?

Rather than getting into a debate about appropriate methods, I kept an open mind. The makeup of the class consisted of different students than previous classes. My topic was also different from other courses. The theories of leadership focus on empowering others. As a principle of life, living what I preach guides my thoughts and respective decisions. How can one teach a course on leadership without leading in the classroom? To me, the lecture format of traditional teaching environments assumes that learners' previous knowledge is irrelevant. The goal of that kind of education is to squeeze as much information into the blank slates of students as you can.[1,2] I was not interested only in managing the classroom. My principle challenged me to consider new approaches to lead the students strategically. After careful consideration, I walked into the class with no set approach. Seeking to understand the unique context of the class, I started with a basic inquiry about their expectations and understanding of leadership. After the first six hours of active exploration, the classroom had been transformed into a safe experiential environment. Going beyond theoretical understanding, students personally experienced the emotions that arise when being "managed," as well as the very different emotions generated when being led and empowered. We stepped outside the classroom and explored different environmental contexts to experience leadership. By the last day of the class, another professor led his class outside the classroom to help learners experience the concepts. Months later, I still get emails from learners sharing how the class had an impact on their life. It was much more than a typical class for them.

Consider the relationships built in this classroom. If I had conformed to conventional practices of lecture—imparting my "wisdom" in a straightforward manner—I may have ended up with the mediocrity of the average class. Instead, the experience built profound relationships with learners. It had a significant influence on my ability to conduct in-depth research for this book. Working with another culture as complex as the Chinese, I concluded that synthesis with patience is the ideal approach.

This example applies to many Westerners going to do business in China. Before going, ample opinions from people and information from books flood your mind on what to do when you arrive. You may have your own ideas that are innovative and unique. If you comply with the external information, it may be the safe route to obtain similar outcomes as others have produced. If you apply your own innovative thoughts, it may be risky but yield profound success or lessons. Which choice do you make? This is often a trick question!

Conventional wisdom calls for duality that forces a choice when it is not necessary. Do you really have to take one approach over another? What if you didn't make a concrete choice? In many situations of unfamiliar foreign contexts, the best choice is not to make one and thus trap yourself into one direction. Keeping an open mind to explore multiple options allows leaders room to synthesize what is best for a given situation with the individuals involved. Due to the uniqueness of individuals involved, no situation may be identical to what others have experienced or books quantify. Behaviorists simplify the complexity of human relationships. If you keep an open mind, you will have more room to maneuver through a given business situation. The skill of synthesis calls for an integration between external information and individual innovation. From an entrepreneurial perspective, synthesis is the source of immense success.

Mastering Synthesis

As you venture into business relationships with the Chinese, are you willing to accept the mediocrity of typical Chinese expectations when working with a Westerner? Or are you willing to explore the contextual richness beyond the surface of behaviorism? In order to be successful, leaders possess a synthesis between self-knowledge and external knowledge. According to many dictionaries, the word synthesis guides a process of combining distinct concepts or elements to create something innovative. It does not completely deny one perspective over another. Instead, it bonds a multiplicity of perspectives to form a complex whole.

The process of synthesis has proliferated in both Western and Chinese philosophy. As early as the days of Plato (427-347 BCE) and Socrates (469-399 BCE), philosophers debated over the concepts of knowledge and how to justify truths. In the history of Western civilizations, the synthesis of knowledge combines many perspectives, such as innate knowledge (Plato and Socrates), empiricism (Hume), rationalism (Descartes), and constructivism (Kant). Plato and Socrates believed that knowledge is innate. Any synthesis of new information starts with internal reflection. Hume, on the other hand, felt that the synthesis of what is real comes from the senses. Descartes introduced the active role that the mind plays in synthesis. Kant rejected both rationalism and empiricism. He felt that we synthesize what we know from realities inside the mind and one derived from the senses.[3] Heidegger comes along and presents hermeneutics. This philosophy is very similar to the synthesis example with the teaching approach towards the Chinese MBA class.

■ MIND GEM 2.1 ■

Mind Gem 2.1: As an innovative business person, you have many innovative thoughts. Working with Chinese leaders, you must be mindful of the relationship context. Often, you may not be too sure where you stand hierarchically or relationally. If you speak outside the boundaries of respect, you may be unknowingly reducing your chances of success. Rather than taking the risk, speak strategically about your idea without stating it. This is similar to playing *Jeopardy*—the popular TV game show where your goal is to state the proper question when shown the answer. Your goal is to lead the Chinese leader to the idea without stating it. This is also a collaborative approach. It stands on a belief that the other person is capable of creating the solution as well. Without the belief, this may appear to be manipulative. Be sure to ask the questions without an attachment of what the answers should be. Combine your innovations with the given answers.

This approach also eliminates the possibility that one might agree with you on the surface save face, but take no action ue to the underlying disagreement. Depending on the relationship context, many [Chinese] will not state concrete disagreement as to Westerners

continued on page 21

Hermeneutics believes in refraining from judgment of a given situation. Reality does not exist in simple dualities and absolutes. Heidegger concluded that knowledge is existential. While the past plays a role, the synthesis of new information is a state of being. Synthesis happens when a conscious and critical mind actively interprets new information in the moment.[3,4]

For example, the ability to speak up and share ideas is one of many leadership traits. In theory, people who are innovative are a crucial part of successful teams. In practice, this is highly dependent on one's hierarchical and political position within an organization as well as individual mental framework and personality. The difference between the theory and practice is entirely another book. The behavior of sharing ideas often is the visible aspect of leadership. Many studies have shown the relationship between innovation and leadership.[5,6] Now going to the other side of the world, sharing ideas is not as simple. The Chinese culture requires a high level of compliance within a hierarchy. People who are in lower positions may embarrass the leaders if they speak up with innovative ideas. If one simply applies the surface of what is visible, a business person may be vocal about innovations in Western society and be silent in Chinese cultures if they do not have the highest positional authority. This practice conforms to the thought that "when in Rome, do as the Romans." Here's the fun part to ponder: if you're traveling halfway around the world, what value do you bring if you remain quiet? At the same time, how would you respect the Chinese culture with your innovative ideas? Heidegger would suggest that there is no absolutism in any given behavior. The duality of speaking up or not is a confining myth, sending many Westerners home without adding sufficient value. A synthesis of the behavior calls for a strategic approach. It does not reject what previous studies have shown. Instead, it considers the outcomes of the past studies from both cultures and creates new models for innovation sharing within each unique situation.

Let's start the journey of synthesis beyond behaviorism with a brief overview of the theoretical foundations.

Theoretical Foundations of the Approach

For many practitioners, the theoretical aspects of tactics may be superfluous information. As an engineer, I understand the practical limitations of such information. Reading this information is far from an efficient use of time on the surface. But as I've progressed in my career and learned from many effective leaders, understanding the theoretical foundations provided the solid rationale for change. It inspired me to think differently, which led to different behaviors and outcomes. Especially when the Chinese ways of doing business are dramatically different from Western perspectives, the changes in behavior may be drastic, along with the thought processes. With any change, there is a natural resistance to change. The theoretical aspects help provide your mind with the rationale it needs to make the changes. It also provides a contextual understanding for skills development. Therefore, the intent to disclosing the foundations of this book is to allow you to develop methods to further your ability to learn about other cultures, not just take the "fish" offered.

The primary theories involved in designing this cultural exploration journey include the synthesis of a wide variety of topics from leadership to psychology. From the leadership body of knowledge, systems thinking,[7] transformational leadership,[6] Socratic methods,[8,9] multiple intelligences,[10] and internalized leadership[11] build the processes within the journey. From the psychology perspective, cognitive psychology,[12] neurolinguistic programming,[13] educational psychology,[1] and organizational psychology[14] provide the

continued from page 20

often do in business. Taking this approach avoids the "surface niceness" challenge.

Tactical steps:

1. Frame the innovative thought in your mind—solidify the content around a specific event. For example, if you have an idea on a new way to produce a product, write it down in detail with diagrams so that it is clear. Let's say you're looking to add one step at the beginning of a project to enhance quality.

2. Applying Socratic methods, create a question funnel with one or two general questions surrounding the event. Then add a few more questions that get at the details around your idea. Using the previous example of the added step, you may create a set of questions related to challenges in the past with quality and what changes may be appropriate from another's perspective.

3. Ask the other party concerning the general event. With the quality issue, ask questions like "How would you describe the quality of the outcome? What would have been ideal?"

continued on page 22

continued from page 21

4. Lead the conversation with follow-up questions such as:
   a. How else would you have approached this . . .?
   b. What will you do differently next time?
   c. What is the underlying issue behind. . . .?

5. Finalize the idea with specifics with questions concerning the timeline, who is involved, and respective resources. Start with the following statements:
   a. This is a great idea.
   b. By when would you be able to accomplish this? How can I help?
   c. What resources are needed?

foundations of understanding the human mind. The synthesis of diverse fields of study creates a different approach to working with different cultures. While the content of various behaviors is interesting and often entertaining, knowing why these practices differ and how to effectively apply strategic thinking around relationships are the keys to working in China or any other nation. As a professor and researcher, the importance of understanding theory is part of the learning. As a practitioner, the theories can get boring, as many textbooks have proven. The key driver that connects the two is how you retain relevant information in this journey. Without a relative permanence in memory, reading the book becomes another form of entertainment. My goal here is to truly empower you to think differently for greater success within any foreign country. To achieve this goal, I will briefly cover some of the theoretical underpinnings of the book. Specific references to key authors/texts are available for further study.

From the business perspective, many theories simply do not apply in China since they are built on Western belief systems such as individualism. When working with Chinese businesspeople, theories such as the agency theory simply do not apply. Agency theory states that people are individualistic. The interests of an individual may override the employer's interests in basic decision-making. Managers attempting to operate under Western beliefs and values will offend many Chinese people and result in significant cultural conflict. Another example is the practice of the 360-degree feedback system. As a theory, it is well accepted in many organizations in the United States. With limited political influences, the feedback from subordinates to managers offers a more balanced approach. In China, blindly applying the 360-degree feedback system results in silence among subordinates, since traditional culture does not permit such direct communication. These and many other business theories in Western business practices are simply irrelevant and possibly offensive if applied to Chinese people, as these concepts are built on content of Western beliefs and values.

On a contextual level, many business concepts/theories have a tremendous impact in working with other people within various situations. Systems thinking is one of the toughest competencies to develop.[7] It challenges people to see everything as systems that are interconnected. The framework reflects a highly complex web of relationships between individuals, teams, organizations, and countries. But working with the Chinese requires such an ability. Success and comprehension comes only after becoming aware of the different system of business and relationships in China.

Transformational leadership is another major Western theory applied to create self-aware leaders who are empowered.[6] From the perspective of this theory, the role of a leader is to transform other people into leaders through five dimensions that include intellectual stimulation and individual consideration. The theory calls for taking the time to understand an individual's needs, rather than placing people into a category. This approach allows people to be inspired for change, rather than be told what to do.

In order to build the most powerful relationships between Western and Chinese leaders, inspiration can be a fuel that launches the business into success. In order to inspire others, knowing another's history and motivations calls for the art of asking questions. Socratic methods provide the methods for that questioning.[8,9] In China, especially with the high level of complexity within the culture and its adaptations of Western practices, taking the time to ask questions to understand the individual enables leaders not to fall into the many cultural myths. With a fundamental belief that human beings are creative entities, the cultural exploration journey uses questions to guide individuals toward being global leaders with transformational awareness.

Multiple intelligences is the final theory in the list of many; it encompasses both leadership and psychology.[10] Multiple intelligences theory enhances one's self-awareness and increases self-esteem. The theory challenges people to think beyond the typical analytical intelligence (IQ) that is a focus of many schools. Within the Chinese culture, key business relationships require much more than analytical intelligence. Other forms of intelligence such as emotional and spiritual intelligence are critical success factors to creating and sustaining meaningful relationships. A popular research topic within multiple intelligences is emotional intelligence.[15] Human beings often make decisions based on their emotions. If one is to be successful working with Chinese leaders, emotional intelligences is a vital part of the relational connection. The Chinese and Western views of emotional intelligence are drastically different. While the Western approach calls for exploring emotional expression, the Chinese culture has limited room for such behaviors, depending on the generation.

The synthesis of these theories creates the foundation for many of the concepts within this book. They are the wheels that carry you through the cultural exploration journey.

From a psychology perspective, cognitive psychology is a scientific approach to learning about the human brain.[12] While the jargon used to name the various parts of the brain may be irrelevant to a practitioner, understanding how the human brain processes information is a starting point for learning. Looking at this personally, your time is crucial. While this book contains an enormous amount of information, constructing it in a way that maintains your attention and helps your recall makes this journey a profouaod return on investment. From a cultural perspective, cognitive psychology also helps people decipher what is short-term and long-term memory. Building effective relationships centers on how you can make a lasting impact in long-term memory. Neurolinguistic programming[13] breaks down human behaviors into a core set of beliefs and values; it also clearly illustrates the band aid approach to most of today's methods of dealing with multicultural issues. The foundation research for this book starts with values and beliefs. Through this *window*, you can see the core of individuals and cultures. Educational psychology serves two purposes.[1] It helps provide the methods to making this book an effective learning tool, while it also influences the strategies that make the most impact on a relationship between Chinese and Western leaders. Finally, organizational psychology is the container that wraps around the other theories. It offers various systems and processes to connect various parts of business. At the core of working with another culture like the Chinese, organizational psychology provides the framework for mastering relationships at multiple levels of business (individual, group, and organization).

A Simple Equation for Learning

Synthesizing the numerous theories for developing the key skills to building effective relationships with Chinese business leaders is a monumental task. The bodies of knowledge from each field contain endless amounts of research. Even after two journeys in doctoral studies in business and psychology, there is still more to learn. The practitioner in me refuses to let the daunting task of combining the rich content of cultures with the abundance of relevant theories deter me. Drawing back on my engineering days, equations are like pictures that say a thousand words. One simple equation that encapsulates the approach to this cultural exploration journey is as follows:

Information + *Emotional attachment* = Profound Knowledge

The information aspect of this book is not like any other on how to do business when in China. There are a number of books with great information on China, although some tend to generalize China as a single culture. This book's content is rich with greater depth of scientific research. The emotional attachment part of the equation is the mental trigger that helps you translate information into knowledge which has permanence in recall and practical application. Looking back at your life, the greatest self-defining lessons come from significant emotional events. Emotions are like a file clerk in your memory. When emotions are high, the associated information gets priority in getting into our limited memory. Borrowing from quantum physics, energy and information are the two basic elements of the world. Emotion is simply *Energy*-in-*Motion*. To build a solid base of competence in international business, understanding and combining the two basic elements helps you become a master of learning. As you journey with us through this book, you will find that there are many activities that create emotional responses. Not all are intended to be easy; if it were easy, everyone would be running to China and making billions. Trust in the activity to bring you to a higher level of awareness as a powerful international leader in business. Consider how you might engage with complete authentic curiosity, free from judgment.

NOTES

1. Jeanne E. Ormrod, *Educational Psychology: Developing Learners* (Upper Saddle River, NJ: Pearson, 2006).
2. Malcolm K. Smith, "Malcolm Knowles, informal adult education, self-direction, and andragogy," the encyclopedia of informal education, www.infed.org/thinkers/et-knowl.htm.
3. Paul K. Moser and Arnold vander Nat, *Human Knowledge: Classical and Contemporary Approaches* (New York: Oxford University Press, 1995).
4. David F. Krell, ed., *Martin Heidegger Basic Writings: from Being and Time (1927) to The Task of Thinking (1964)* (New York: HarperCollins, 1993).
5. Gregory T. Lumpkin and Gregory G. Dess, "Clarifying the Entrepreneurial Orientation Construct and Linking It to Performance," *Academy of Management Review* 21 (1996): 135–73.
6. Bernard M. Bass, *Bass & Stogdill's Handbook of Leadership*, 3rd ed. (New York: Free Press, 1990).
7. Peter Checkland, *Systems Thinking, Systems Practice: A 30 year Retrospective* (New York: John Wiley & Sons, Inc., 1999).
8. Richard Paul and Linda Elder, "Critical Thinking: The Art of Socratic Questioning," *Journal of Developmental Education* 31(1) (Fall 2007): 36–37.
9. Aaron A. Tucker, Leadership by the Socratic Method. *Air & Space Power Journal* 21(2) (Summer 2007): 80–87.
10. Howard Gardner, *Multiple Intelligences: The Theory in Practice* (New York: Basic Books, 1993).
11. Ted Sun, *Survival Tactics: Top 11 Behaviors of Successful Entrepreneur* (Westport, CT: Greenwood Publishing Group, 2007).
12. Robert J. Sternberg, *Cognitive Psychology*, 4th ed. (Belmont, CA: Thomson Wadsworth, 2006).
13. Steve Bavister and Amanda Vickers, *Teach Yourself NLP* (Chicago: Contemporary Books, 2004).
14. Frank L. Landy and Jeffrey M. Conte, *Work in the 21st Century: An Introduction to Industrial and Organizational Psychology* (New York: McGraw Hill Companies, 2004).
15. Robert K. Cooper and Ayman Sawaf, *Executive EQ: Emotional Intelligence in Business* (New York: Berkley Publishing Group, 1998).

Business Context
in the West

The context of business is like an engine underneath a car. On the surface, the "cars" of businesses all focus on revenues, profits, and market share. What is enabling the car to go fast or slow with maneuverability is a hidden context often forgotten. By contrasting economic and belief systems, we'll explore the drastic differences between Western and Chinese cultures. We in the West tend to think that we all know so well the economic context of China through our many studies and data. Yet, beneath all the studies, Western eyes are trained to see life from one perspective, while China's perspective is quite different. Gaining clarity concerning the Western business perspective provides insight into what's really causing some of the issues that we face today, such as the global economic crisis.

Unseen to most people, the Western business context of capitalism speeds past many developing countries and theorists. On the visible side, the car is loaded with "pretty" characteristics like color, shape, style, and sound. With a highly developed left brain interpreter, content-based logical systems dominate and reduce reality to simple cause and effects.

The left brain interpreter is a part of your brain that is responsible for making you feel good about the decisions you make. Its purpose is to create reasons for every action and decision. In neurobiological studies, experiments induced artificial movements. In one study, the researchers placed an electrical stimulus on the part of the brain that would make a person stand up. Before introducing the stimulus, the researchers ensured that the participant was perfectly comfortable with absolutely no need for anything. They then introduced the small electric charge that made the participant stand up. When he did, the researchers ask the participant why. Without the slightest hesitation, the participant manufactured a reason for standing up. He replied,

"I was thirsty and wanted to get a drink of water." While the researchers realized the flaw of this reasoning since the participant only stood up and didn't move towards the water fountain, they also proved the brilliance of the left brain interpreter in its capabilities to create a reason for any decision to allow the human mind to believe in its ability to be in control.[1]

The Context of the "Economic Crisis"

Moving the content-based logic system into reality, regarding the economic crisis that started in 2008 and into 2009, most point their finger to the subprime mortgage markets. They feel that the large number of foreclosures upset the balance in credit markets. This led to an unstable global financial market.[2] Looking at this from another perspective, we learn that sources from the FBI claim that the financial crisis was sparked by an exponential increase in fraudulent activities, especially in the mortgage industry.[3] Another perspective points to the outsourcing trend as a major influence that caused the many foreclosures that led to the financial crisis. While all of these reasons make sense, they place certain parties at the center of attention. While there's no doubt that both could have played a role in the crisis, the surface view of the situation is too simple. This is merely the visible side of the capitalism car.

Under the visible glamour and ugliness, the current state of organizations is much more complex. Going beyond the hood of the economic crisis, many contextual processes drove the business cycle. On the surface, some blame President George W. Bush for the economic conditions. Yet, it was President Clinton who cleared the way through policy, allowing many high-risk people to own homes. On one hand, there was the optimistic glamour of having many more Americans own homes. This included many minorities whose ownership would help move them into the middle class. On the other hand, there was a strategic political move involved that ensured a large voting bloc and returned favors to political allies. The new policy rewrote mortgage industry rules and enabled high-risk homeownership. This 1993 decision created the context for the subprime market.[4] As you are reading this, you might be thinking that this could be the root cause of the issue. Your left brain interpreter wants something concrete so that it is simple to understand. Unfortunately, it is much more complicated than this single decision by a president.

One of the most fascinating aspects of politics and economics is the lack of truth shared by politicians. While many like to take the credit for economic success or deny blame for economic fallouts, political figures (not necessarily leaders) are not sharing the entire truth. It would be brilliant and incredibly courageous to have a president step up and share with the people how the business cycle operates. Within the Western context of business, the drivers for success or crisis follow supply and demand. While political decisions have an influence, there are many other drivers in this complex system.

For example, the trend of outsourcing is a result of high wages and low unemployment. America cannot stay at a low unemployment rate all the time. With low unemployment rates, people have ample job opportunities and demand a high salary. This high salary does not allow firms to be competitive in a world marketplace. On the other hand, a rise in unemployment rates lowers salaries since more people have a desperate need to work. They will work for lower salaries, which potentially brings jobs back. Unfortunately, there has never been a politician who would have the courage to educate the public on basic economic principles and inform the public of how they work. Perhaps, it is too cumbersome of a task with the hours of media exposure. Operating with a *fear-driven mentality*, an abundance of *quick fixes* populates the toolboxes of many leaders.[5] Perhaps it is much easier to point the figure at someone than to look for the root cause. Maybe it is the expense of airtime that prevents politicians from taking the time to educate the public about the business cycle. Of course, that would be blaming the politicians. An empowered view would call for each person to get educated not by the media, but by learning the solid fundamental theories of macro- and microeconomics.

As I'm writing these thoughts, I wondered how simple it would be for an average individual to get online and find this information. I typed in "business cycle" at both Yahoo and Google. Both pulled up Wikipedia as the number one source. (From an academic perspective, most higher education institutions discourage or prohibit using this as a source of information, since it lacks research foundations and contains false information.) Most of the sites from the search touch on the basic concepts. One missing element is the illustration of a cycle using supply and demand curves. Most show an economics movement like a sine wave with ups and downs. Venturing further in my quest for an internet source, I added the search terms "supply and demand." I was able to pull up a site from the University of Colorado that fully detailed the actual business cycle in both text and illustrations.[6] Knowing the key words is essential, which might present a challenge for the average person in the quest to obtain the key information. Perhaps, on a systemic level, politicians and organizational leaders can provide some guidance for the general public to educate themselves.

This leads us into a challenging thought: The context of business is much more complex than simple cause-and-effect. How do we move a general population interested in quick answers and simple cause-and-effect rationale towards an interest in understanding the business context? The current economic crisis is just part of the business cycle that comprises many variables on a macro level. Knowing how it works, one can make millions during times of crisis; the major challenge is predicting the duration of the cycle. History has shown that the last major depressions made millionaires of those who were able to see the context and not think within scarcity boundaries. Part of working on an international level makes this potential more significant. Being able to see the context is highly profitable. I've embedded some of these contextual opportunities throughout the book; they are for you to profit.

Understanding Business Context

The business context is a complex web of systems. Perceiving these systems is a skill that mirrors one's ability to see the individual trees from the forest. It calls for a slowing down of quick judgments and quick fixes. Events do not happen because something is out to get you or because you get lucky. Events don't happen to you; they occur with you as part of the system. The ability to see the system at work empowers strategic decisions at the foundational level, rather than the surface level.

Three Components of Context: Individual, Society, and Systemic Interactions

The context of business environments has three major components. The first is the individual system. Within this system, a complex web of multiple intelligences drives one's perceptions of reality. The fundamental building blocks are one's beliefs and values systems.[7,8] Through these building blocks, events occurring in the external world drive specific perceptions.[9] For example, when stuck in a traffic jam, what perceptions run through your mind? Many people have a victim perception: "Why me?" Others may see it as an opportunity to slow down to reflect on the day. Some may even extend their concern for the people in the accident ahead and wish them well. These three interpretations illustrate one's thinking driven by beliefs about self and values like efficiency and empathy.

Within the individual system, one major consideration is the importance of treating people as individuals and not labeling them by race, color, ethnic background, or any surface marker. And assumptions about what it means to be an American or a Chinese are far too general in the minds of most people. Nor is the practice of making assumptions very profitable. Making a conscious choice to see the individual sends a contextual message that he or she is important and unique. This approach requires a high level of awareness of—and wariness of—simplistic judgments driven by the left brain interpreter.[1] With great effort, the focus on understanding the individual yields incredible rewards in business, especially when working with Chinese business leaders who focus on the importance of relationship. As you seek to understand their diverse and unique experiences, combined with a mixture of traditional Eastern beliefs and values with Western influences, the journey becomes a contextual goal crucial for success.

My desire to learn more about the individual system drove me to research the area of beliefs and values and present my findings in this book. While there is extensive literature concerning differences between Western and Eastern beliefs, research on values is rather limited. Furthermore, most of the research generalizes people at the national level. Researchers fail to seek understanding of specific regions in a country, genders, or generations. The following Web site provides the scientific data for this book. You are welcome to explore this survey instrument for yourself or go further to explore the congruence of individuals and organizations:

www.InternationalValuesStudy.org

The second component has to do with society. Within each society, there is a set list of norms and guidelines defined by a culture.[10] The culture is one perspective on the context of business. In Western business environments, for example, a set of contracts typically guides transactions and sets clear expectations. Cultures can often dictate the appropriate behaviors and challenge one's personal values systems. A culture can also include a set of implicit rules in the "game" of business. Patterns of thought and responses are also part of one's culture. All of these dimensions make the societal component complex, since it involves behaviors, emotions, and cognitive processes that contain individuals.

The final context of interest is the systemic interactions. The culture of a given society is the system within which many interactions take place. Edgar Schein, a renowned leader of organizational psychology at the MIT Sloan School of Management, distinguishes leaders and managers through their ability to change culture. He believes that leaders are able to create and change culture consciously, while managers and administrators simply live within a culture. [11] Applying this principle to the economic crisis, many politicians work within the given culture to place blame in a simple cause-and-effect relationship. They choose to perceive a surface level set of interactions. Conspiracy theorists may even call these practices a method of keeping people in the dark so that they can be easily controlled. Sharing the knowledge concerning the economic crisis from a business cycle context would call for significant courage. This leadership could shift a society based on surface-level content towards a culture of systemic thinkers who see the context.

On the other hand, placing blame within the powers of a limited few does not empower individuals to act on their own within the numerous interactions. The societal norm influences finger pointing at a positional figure. The individual system can depart from that norm, look at oneself, and realize the role one has played in this. Whether it's the finger pointing or a reflection within self, the business context is loaded with interactions between individuals within a society.

From a theoretical foundation, this book takes an approach that any individual has the potential to shift and lead cultures or business norms. This fact leads us to the third component of business context—the interaction between the individual leader (that's you) and the societal norms. While the previous Web site provided the data from an individual perspective of self-reflection, the following exercise illustrates your perception of the drivers for the American business context. How you perceive the reality that you live in influences the choices you make. This brief quiz reveals your perceptions of the American business culture.

The American Business Context Quiz

This quiz is a quick assessment of your knowledge concerning the business context of Americans. There are no right or wrong answers to these questions. Simple fill out what you believe to be your experiences. Once you have finished, read on to see what our study found.

Table 2.0 Jot down what you believe are the top five values that drive American businesspeople.

Top Five Values

1.
2.
3.
4.
5.

Table 2.1 Circle what you see as the level of importance for each belief (6 being very high and 1 being very low). For example, in your experience, how much do Americans believe in a life purpose?

Belief	Low	Medium			High	
Life purpose	1	2	3	4	5	6
Power distance (hierarchy)	1	2	3	4	5	6
Loyalty and concern for community	1	2	3	4	5	6
Being proactive	1	2	3	4	5	6
Individualism	1	2	3	4	5	6
Importance of relationships	1	2	3	4	5	6
Trust of foreigners	1	2	3	4	5	6

Table 2.2 How important are these concepts to American businesspeople?

Concept	Not too Important		Medium		Very Important	
Family	1	2	3	4	5	6
Honesty	1	2	3	4	5	6

Table 2.3 How congruent do you believe American businesspeople to be (%, with 100% being perfectly congruent, meaning that their actions are in alignment with their beliefs and values system)? _____%

The answers to the quiz will be spread out in the book according to their relevance. One dimension of interest is the level of congruence. Congruence is people's ability to live in a manner aligned with their core values and beliefs. This is one of the root causes for the increasing stress in people's lives. For example, if you believe in fairness, a congruent behavior would be to provide people the chance to have input into a decision that involves them. While that's easy to theorize, most organizational systems are still hierarchical. They pass down decisions from leaders with very limited, if any, involvement from lower-level employees. The battle for successful implementation challenges one's belief about being fair.

Levels of Congruence within Context

Our study looked at two dimensions of congruence. The first is one's congruence with core values. The second is the congruence with core beliefs. While there is a large set of core beliefs, the study included beliefs about life purpose, power distance, individualism, relationships, trust, and success. Within the dimension of values congruence, fascinating but reasonable outcomes appeared. Within the sample of business leaders from across America, the overall level of congruence with the top eight values was 0.595 (or 60%). The Chinese data illustrated a higher value, 71.1%. (This number is the Pearson correlation coefficient between one's determination of importance on specific values and the ability to behave accordingly.) If people were able to be perfect, the relationship between the two would yield a 1.0 for the Pearson correlation coefficient. Interestingly, the state of Ohio has a high level of congruence on values with 59.9%. East Coast states have slightly lower congruence at 46.1%. Although this aspect alone could be a book dedicated to understanding these differences between regions, the focus of this book resides with understanding self and achieving successful relationships with Chinese business leaders. Aside from the statistical definitions, a congruence of 59.5% illustrates the existing challenges facing the American people. When people have a set of core values but they are not able to live within those values, it creates a significant level of internal dissonance. This is a contextual challenge that leads to many forms of mental and physical illness.

CONGRUENCE OF FAMILY
AND HONESTY

Digging deeper into the values congruence, the importance of family was the top value of Americans. Out of the 63 values in the list, family received 11.56% of the total points. The next closest one, integrity, was 8.21%. This clearly illustrates the desire of Americans to create a strong family unit. After nearly a decade of doing leadership-related workshops, work-life balance has always been one of the top well-attended topics. This wasn't simply due to a high significance of the family value; there was also something missing in most people's lives. The study found that people were only able to achieve a congruence of 64.88%. This is a clear reflection that haunts many organizations in their attempt to balance the organizational needs with family needs.

One specific value that's crucial and appears to be at the top of behavior conversation is the degree of honesty. While I was working with a group of adult MBA students who were executives and managers, one of the perceptions of Americans by Chinese business leaders was a high degree of honesty. One student, a human resource executive, stated, "Americans are too honest. They tell you too much." While this was the perception, does it really match how Americans view themselves? Putting this into context, the Chinese perspective sees Americans as straightforward concerning many topics, and not hesitant to disagree. From the American cultural perspective, freedom of speech gives you the right to share your thoughts. When this value showed up as the fourth most important value, I decided to look further into it. The detailed analysis revealed a congruence level of 68.57%. This figure illustrates the clear desire for people to be very honest. In an ideal situation, people prefer to share their thoughts, ideas, and opinions. In reality, the current structures within the business context leave room for improvement. In the countless workshops with organizational leaders, honesty is one of the most challenging ideologies. Many barriers get in the way of being honest. For some, it's the fear of legal action; for others, it's the fear of the emotional response. We live in a culture where norms dictate behaviors that do not hurt people's feelings. In this paradigm, people often don't get to learn key lessons from honest disclosure.

In consideration of honesty, one crucial aspect to embody is the platinum rule for respect. Notice it's not the typical golden rule that many people still preach and believe. We've all heard the golden rule—"Do unto others as you would like to be done unto you." While this may function well within a homogeneous population, it creates many challenges in a diverse workplace. The platinum rule for respect guides thought in consideration of others in their thoughts. It states: "Do unto others as they would like to be done unto them." This enhancement shifts the center of thought away from self and onto another. A few years ago, I heard a keynote speaker on leadership preach the golden rule at a graduation ceremony. After the ceremony, I approached the speaker and asked him if he would be open to some feedback (establish the context) in the midst of many congratulatory comments from others. After agreement, I opened the dialog by asking for clarification in his intent with the golden rule on respect. The individual quickly reiterated the conventional thought. While he did that, I slowed my mind down to consider how I might be able to reach him (a contextual focus) and empower him to create a more healthy focus in his future talks. I then asked, "How many people in this room are exactly like you and have the same values or expectations for behaviors as you do?" The question slowed down in his mind. He looked around for a moment and responded, "Not too many; we're all unique individuals." I realized that he was on the brink of a significant realization. I proceeded to ask, "So if we are to apply this rule to decisions and behaviors, how might that cause some major challenges?" This led to a further discussion of the conventional thought and the creation of a new rule for respect.

I understand that it was a huge challenge to approach a keynote speaker with constructive feedback. While it may be out of the ordinary, the long-term perspective is the potential harm he could do when people applied his views without conscious awareness of its limitations. I understood that I had many traditional barriers in appearance and hierarchy. The man had gray hair and explicit accomplishments. I have dark hair and a youthful appearance. The man was also a keynote speaker; to him, I was simply an audience member. You may even think about the norm of "not embarrassing" someone. Regardless of the barriers, the efforts were part of the experiment in integrity. I needed to be congruent with my sense of honesty and to provide feedback in a way that a leader can hear it and have a chance to apply it authentically. In this case, he heard my argument and changed his approach in future speaking engagements.

CONGRUENCE OF BELIEFS

Uncovering beliefs required taking a different route in the study. While values assessment started with a comprehensive list of 63 values that participants narrowed to the top eight, a beliefs list would have to have been significantly longer. As a result, the study focused on 13 specific beliefs that would greatly influence international business. They included basic beliefs about who's in charge (power) and view of self along with one's role in society. The assessments contained 13 beliefs. Beliefs such as life purpose, power distance, individualism, role of relationships, and success influence many behaviors within human dynamics. Rather than using one single measurement (scale) like most other studies,

◼ MIND GEM 2.2 ◼

Mind Gem 2.2: Honesty is a tough game of balance. How can you be honest so that the relationship reflects trust and long-term growth for both parties? How can you avoid the immediate emotional reactions that may not align with cultural norms of not hurting another's feelings? Especially with a culture that needs to show respect (save face), sharing relevant information takes on a strategic approach. The following is one approach that allows you to step around the rigid norms and delicate feelings of people. It first looks at the relationship—the connector between you and the other person. It then looks at the self-system to ensure authenticity towards the greater good. Finally, it strategically configures the information.

Tactical steps:

1. Understand the context of the relationship.
   a. In Western cultures, you can simply ask the other person if they would like to have a perfectly open and honest relationship, or if the person wants feedback.
   b. In Chinese cultures, that line of question may only

continued on page 36

continued from page 35

get you what is most agreeable depending on the perceived hierarchical position. So you will need to look at past engagements with the person, while also considering other factors that may influence this such as generational aspects, regional characteristics, and adaptation to Western approaches.

2. Assess the information in your own mind. Before sharing information, ask yourself the following questions. These questions help you understand if the information you wish to share comes from an authentic you, and not one driven by ego, which wants to beat others down with criticism so you can feel good about yourself.

   a. Does this piece of information help me or the other person?

   b. What is my intent in sharing the information?

3. Design the approach to be easily absorbed. This is probably one of the most challenging areas for most people. While we all contain valuable information, how we communicate

continued on page 37

I used a two-perspective measurement. The first perspective studied the degree of importance concerning beliefs; the second sought to understand the level of behavior alignment with the level of importance. While the discussion concerning values has a hierarchical order of eight, the beliefs discussion does not have an explicit order of priorities. The focus of this section is to provide a high-level overview of beliefs and respondents' congruence with them. Later chapters will explore the commonalities of beliefs between the Chinese and Americans.

On the beliefs dimension, the level of congruence is at 0.541 or 54.1%. It was rather interesting to see a lower congruence with beliefs compared to values. The Chinese results stood at 58.5%. While these numbers provide interesting information, they are far from being conclusive, nor do they apply to every individual. Digging further, comparisons between regions and gender also revealed some fascinating information. In America, the levels of congruence appear to be higher in the Midwest (57.8%) compared to the East Coast (43.0%). Males tend to have higher levels of congruence at 67.2% compared to females at 51.4%.

As you are reading these numbers, observe your mind as it celebrates outcomes favorable to your group while perhaps rejecting the numbers if you are in the lower group. As discussed before, your left brain interpreter[1] will automatically do its job in making you feel good. The intent of sharing this information is not to categorize one group over another. It merely illustrates the complexity of statistics and how it cannot contain humanity. A statistical number does not represent a human being.[12] We can easily continue to dissect the data into generational comparisons, ethnic groups, educational backgrounds, professional achievements, socioeconomic classes, and so on. The list of categories is endless and provides significant employment for statisticians. The challenge is to be conscious of the uniqueness of each individual and let these numbers be permeable boundaries, rather than rigid boxes that contain any group.

Definition of Success

The definition of success drives many behaviors and decisions in life. This is both a simple and complex topic. It is simple from the perspective that many people assume one dimension to success in conversations and journeys. It is complex as deeper conversations yield an emotional and a spiritual dimension. Throughout Western cultures, the desire to be successful meant different tangible goals at various stages of development. As a child, being successful meant that you listened to adults (a form of conformity). As a student, success was based on achievement of grades or athletic accomplishments. Success for an adult becomes more complex with an overwhelming expectation for financial freedom. I've often had a great time challenging leaders to think beyond the programmed definition of success and redefine it within one's passion.

Is success something artificial like money, a house, or cars? Or is success something intrinsic such as feelings of happiness or gratification? Is there a spiritual element to it as well?

Since success is the finish line that people reach for, understanding the beliefs about success facilitates the understanding of people in relationships. In a previous study of successful entrepreneurs, intangible success factors (gratification, happiness, fulfillment, independence) outweighed tangible factors (profits, revenues) by 24.4%. This provided a basis for a definition of success as it clearly revealed the focus of successful people. In a field where over 80% of entrepreneurs fail within five years, the successful ones focus more on intrinsic goals for success.

Within the current study, new dimensions of success included emotional and spiritual dimensions, in addition to the tangible aspect. From the leaders surveyed,

continued from page 36

this information makes a world of difference. Regardless of cultures, determine the best approach for the other person to accept and embrace this information. The "how you say it" aspect is a vital element in communication. It is another contextual consideration for powerful relationships. In this context, Socratic methods can be very powerful tools. Rather than simply stating the information, help the other person realize the information on their own by asking questions. This will allow the other person the chance to own that information. Especially in the Chinese culture, where open disagreement would harm the relationship, asking questions helps you understand and navigate the delicate context. Basic questions lead the other person towards understanding on their own:

a. How would you proceed in this situation?

b. What are some factors (leading to missing pieces that the other does not see) that we've not identified?

the degree of importance placed on financial gains was the lowest (4.58 out of 6). Happiness (5.14) and career satisfaction (5.11) were the top two success measures. One's life purpose scored a 4.95. Understanding the goals that one seeks to achieve helps facilitate collaborative strategies. At the same time, knowing where you are in the journey currently reveals the starting point. The self-perceptions of achievement were surprising in our sample. Happiness appeared as the lowest level of achievement at 32%. Financial success achievement was close behind at 39%. These two aspects reflected the current mentality of many Americans from an emotional and logical perspective. On the other hand, the satisfaction with career and achievement of life purpose showed higher scores of 53% and 57% respectively. Since both of these are long-term perspectives, it provides evidence that people generally are more confident in their spiritual journeys.

The context of Western business practices resides on a core set of values and beliefs. Each has its role in driving behaviors and decisions. Whether it's one's value of honesty or a belief about success, the biggest and most exciting challenge is the journey of discovery at the individual level. Within the context of a global economy, assumptions about another person based on their nationality, gender, skin color, or other categories will result in conflicts. Even within Western societies, ample conflicts arise from a lack of understanding and an abundance of categorization. Your journey to be an incredibly successful, international business leader is to understand yourself and individuals from other cultures. This chapter provides some insights on the possible context of your environment. With a developed insight into your existing context, you are empowered to lead by making systemic shifts, such as sharing contextual knowledge with others. It is also a fundamental building block to construct a collaborative context of business with China or any other culture. With this information, I leave you with one thought to explore:

What is the context that I live in today?

NOTES

1. Michael S. Gazzaniga, *The Mind's Past* (Berkeley, CA: University of California Press, 1998).
2. "Subprime meltdown," Investopedia, http://www.investopedia.com/terms/s/subprime-meltdown.asp.
3. Justin Blum, "'Exponential Rise' in Mortgage Fraud Seen by FBI," Bloomberg.com, http://www.bloomberg.com/apps/news?pid=20601103&sid=aitpF.1mEoTc&refer=us.
4. Terry Jones, "How a Clinton-Era Rule Rewrite Made Subprime Crisis Inevitable," IBD Editorials, http://www.ibdeditorials.com/IBDArticles.aspx?id=307149667289804.
5. Dave Baker, Cathy Greenberg, and Collins Hemingway, *What Happy Companies Know: How The New Science of Happiness Can Change Your Company for the Better* (Upper Saddle River, NJ: Pearson Prentice Hall, 2006).

6. "The Business Cycle, Aggregate Demand and Aggregate Supply," The University of Colorado, http://www.colorado.edu/Economics/courses/econ2020/section7/section7-main.

7. Steve Bavister and Amanda Vickers, *Teach yourself NLP* (Chicago: Contemporary Books, 2004).

8. Ted Sun, "Leading Sustainable Change through Self-Discovery" (paper presented at the United Nations Global Forum: Business as an Agent of World Benefit: Management Knowledge Leading Positive Change, Case Western Reserve University, January 4, 2007). http://www.executive-balance.com/UNLeadingSustainableChange.

9. Ted Sun, *Survival Tactics: Top 11 Behaviors of Successful Entrepreneurs* (Westport, CT: Greenwood Publishing Group, 2007).

10. Edgar H. Schein, *The Corporate Culture Survival Guide* (San Francisco: Jossey-Bass, 1999).

11. Edgar H. Schein, *Organizational Culture and Leadership* (San Francisco: Jossey-Bass, 1992).

12. Carl. G. Jung, *The Undiscovered Self* (New York: Penguin Group Inc., 1958).

Business Context in China

Many books on doing business in China discuss appropriate behaviors; very few of them discuss the contextual aspect of business. Unfortunately, the conventional practice of diversity has many authors focus on the differences between cultures. While the differences are important, the synthesis of cultures starts at commonalities. It is often easier to discuss Confucian principles of life and American virtues. It is much more difficult to first discover and then to write about the commonalities of context between the two cultures. On one hand, sharing the principles of Confucianism provides insight into Chinese history as well as rules for life. On the other hand, how does it relate to Western views and the synthesis of the two cultures?

The attempt to compare Chinese and American cultures is like comparing apples and carrots. The concept of apples and oranges still holds the context of tree fruits. The choice to use apples and carrots illustrates a difference in the context of growth. One grows above ground on a tree while the other grows in the ground. The two cultures are drastically different, with significantly different histories. While American history is young (only a few hundred years), it is a collage of many cultures that migrated to America, from the colonial era through today. Chinese culture is grounded in thousands of years of tribes and wars. Furthermore, ample innovation and an ability to adapt litter the culture throughout its history. Yet rather than sharing the content of the cultures and featuring their differences, we start with a common basis of values and beliefs that drives both cultures.

■ MIND GEM 2.3 ■

Mind Gem 2.3: Is it fair to compare apples and carrots? As I'm presenting the numbers regarding values, the Western context of comparison keeps sneaking into my mind. Just because one culture has a higher level of congruence, it doesn't make one better than another. Congruence is not about a competition between people. Each individual has his or her own journey. The level of congruence can also be a hidden bomb. A culture of compliance can yield high levels of congruence, but towards what values?

Be conscious of the need to compare, since this is a natural thought process of the left brain interpreter. One of the basic principles of Confucians, and a prized value among many Chinese today, is inner harmony. An individual cannot have inner harmony when there's a constant comparison with the outside world leading towards some judgment.

Tactical steps:

1. When you find yourself comparing, ask yourself the following questions:
   a. Am I looking to make a conclusion?
   b. Am I making categories out of people?

continued on page 43

Chinese Business Context—Values and Congruence

Using the same three components of context from the previous chapter (the individual, society, and systemic interactions), the individual system is very diverse. On a macro-level, most Chinese people value health over all other values. This is consistent with China's primary goal in modernization to feed and clothe its people.[1] From a historical perspective, the basic necessities have been a significant challenge with a huge population spread out across the country. Since World War II, the new Communist government realized the challenges of the vast population. The lack of resources to feed and clothe its people would lead to significant civil unrest. The one-child policy hoped to control population growth so that all Chinese could have sufficient food and clothing. Looking back, the challenges dating back from the 1950s through the 1970s continue to dominate the primary value of the Chinese people. Comparatively, the value of health was within the top five for most people, but it was not the top value among Westerners. With the top value being different between the Chinese and Westerners, the individual system's thought process will be unique to that top value.

In the Chinese portion of the study, the level of congruence to values is high. Overall, congruence with all of the selected values had a range from 48.1% on the low end to 83.3% on the high end. The American data set had a lower range of 38.3% to 80.9%. Ironically, the value of honesty did not make the top eight values as it did in the American results. Instead, the Chinese had many values that did not exist in the American value set like career success, personal achievement, competence, love of competition, and inner harmony. The Chinese also have an overall congruence to values of 66.5% compared to the American congruence of 64.9%.

The value of love for family also existed in the top eight. Depending on the region, gender, and generation, family had its highest point as the second value and its lowest point as the seventh value. As Americans continue to struggle with work-life balance with a congruence value of 68.88%, the Chinese also share the challenge (at 71.9%).

Traditionally, the Chinese culture was mostly an agrarian state. The family unit was the basic unit of organization and work. To be successful, the family extended key relationships towards the community in order to share scarce resources.[3] When a family lacked a resource, family members were able to leverage other relationships such as friends into a wide network of community resources. Such requests and easy access into community resources are extremely efficient (a day or two in most cases) when the strength of the relationship is strong, much more so than in Western societies (a week or longer in most cases). Compared to many Western societies where the individual is the basic unit of work, Confucius further extended the concept of family into the moral fiber of Chinese society.

The struggle to survive and generational differences move family up and down within the priority of values. Within the Anhui province, the value of career edged out family as a higher value. In the city of Beijing, the value of family is the number two value, while career is number six. Generational gaps also make a significant difference. For people who were born after the 1980s, family was tied with two other values (comfort and cooperation). For people who were born before the 1980s, family stands as a strong value, being second on the priority list. From a gender perspective, males rated family as the third most important while females rated it second. The varying priority placement on family illustrates the shifts from the traditions of Chinese culture. Someone who places career before family may yield very

continued from page 42

c. Is my ego looking for self-gratification?

If the answer to any of the above is yes, slow down and be conscious of this behavior. Don't attempt to fight it or stop it. This will only focus on the negative. Instead, embrace your thought process as a natural phenomenon. The awareness of making comparisons opens the possibility to different realities.

2. After you've made the comparisons and/or come to a conclusion, ask yourself these questions:

a. How might I miss some intricacies of an individual when I group people?

b. What other dimensions are missing from this comparison?

c. How does competitive thought limit my thinking?

d. Does the past predict the future?

These questions are intended to engage your mind. There is no right or wrong answer to them. It helps you reflect and be more aware of common practices, which is part of the journey to understand the Chinese culture.

different behaviors in the workplace compared with those who place family first. Regardless of the value, it is near impossible to completely categorize one person with a given set of priorities.

Chinese Business Context—Beliefs and Congruence

Belief systems make up the second half of the business context. One belief, the concept of self-efficacy, defines one's own capability to reach specific goals, execute specific behaviors, or learn certain skills.[2] Those with a high sense of self-efficacy tend to be entrepreneurial. Believing in self, they take on more challenging tasks, resulting in greater learning and growth regardless of the outcomes. This is one common basis for action that Chinese and Americans share. Both cultures ranked self-efficacy as one of the more important beliefs (Chinese at 4.65 and Americans at 4.84). While both valued self-efficacy, Americans (at 63.0%) had higher levels of congruence than the Chinese had (at 36.31%). One of the possible reasons for such a lower level of congruence in the Chinese for self-efficacy is their journey towards prosperity. While Americans have enjoyed decades of prosperity, China is just beginning its journey. The overall level of congruence on beliefs is 38.22%. This is significantly lower than the American level (54.1%).

How are you doing with your awareness of comparisons and your resulting judgments? While this is a very tough challenge, the numbers are just numbers. It does not make one culture better or more advanced than another. They simply are just numbers that guide more exploration. The normal Western practice is to compare/compete oneself to/with another. But is that really necessary? No one person is the same as another. Looking at the Confucian way of life, the interconnections and interdependencies of life challenge Chinese people to look inward for growth, rather than at external comparisons. The interconnectedness of people is a fundamental belief that has similarities with the federalist realities of American history before the Industrial Revolution.[3,4] Many Chinese people carry this belief, which results in a high focus on harmonious relationships with other people. Often, if your mind is consumed with comparisons with other people or organizations, the resulting relationship will lack trust and collaboration. Since the fiber of China is relationships, working to minimize making constant comparisons will be a continued journey woven throughout this book.

Another fascinating item is the level of belief congruence between males and females. In China, the level of overall congruence is significantly higher in females (64.32%) than in males (58.16%) within the 13 measured beliefs. One possible rationale for this could be the propensity for Chinese males to be very self-critical. From a business perspective, the level of self-assessment within Chinese males could lead towards powerful growth. Consistent with other studies such as that of the Hay Group, it has been found with Chinese CEOs that the desire for self-improvement provides an empowering perspective at both the individual and organizational level.[5] This is also another reason why Socratic methods are very effective. Rather than telling a Chinese leader you disagree and potentially causing them to lose face, asking a few open-ended questions provides rich content for reflection. Ironically, the American gender congruence is exactly the opposite, with the males at 67.2% and females at 51.4%. These differences could lead towards a fascinating study on gender and congruence.

Chinese Business Context—Defining Success

The concept of success in China is holistic. It does not only involve one's salary or career; it includes many other aspects such as physical health, relationships, and professional achievements. The study found no distinct measure for success. Instead, there was a relatively even balance between tangible factors and intrinsic emotions. Overall, financial success had the lowest level of importance at 4.02 (out of 6). Happiness and career satisfaction had higher levels of importance at 4.53 and 4.46 respectively. All of the success factors were within a small range. When it comes to the levels of achievement, the financial success measure had the lowest percentage (9.97%) based on level of importance and perceived achievement. This reflects China's ambitions for itself and its people. While financial success demonstrates a very critical level of achievement, happiness appears to be untouched. Within the American dataset, the levels of achievement in happiness and financial success are both at the thirtieth percentile. In contrast, the Chinese may see worse levels (9.97%) in achievement in financial success, but still feel happy at 36.55%. And in some cities like Anhui, the happiness achievement is at 48.3% with a financial achievement score of 30.52%. Shanghai, on the other hand, had the highest level of financial success at 33.69%, but the lowest level of happiness at 7.69%. One very interesting aspect from the study found an inverse relationship between an individual's perceived achievement of success and the size of the city. As the cities increased in size, the level of perceived achievement became lower (see table 2.3.1).

The results become more distinct when looking at the younger generation in the workplace (the 1980s generation: people under 30 but over 18 years old). For this generation, they view their achievement of happiness to be at 76.41%, the highest in any group or region. At the same time, they assess their financial success at a low 14.60%. This ability to detach happiness with finances marks a significant difference in the approach to business for Chinese people. This is also consistent with the Confucius principle around profits. As he states, "If one's acts are motivated by profits, he will have many enemies."[6] In looking at the different generations' perspectives on success (see table 2.3.2), all three generations rated happiness as more important than finances or career.

Many of these unique beliefs in the Chinese business context come from Confucian philosophy. According to Confucius, "Lead the people with

Table 2.3.1. Success achievement comparison between regions.

Region	Overall Success Achievement (%)
Anhui	30.95
Beijing	24.16
Shanghai	19.54

governmental measures and regulate them by law and punishment, and they will avoid wrongdoing but have no sense of honor and shame. Lead them with virtue and regulate them by the rules of propriety, and they will have a sense of shame and, moreover, set themselves right."[5] While Confucius (551 BCE to 495 BCE) lived well before the time of Western philosophers like Plato and Socrates, the first portion of his statement resembles the content-driven society of American business and way of life. Within this context, ample rules and regulations attempt to contain people's ethical boundaries with punishments. Within the Chinese business context, it is far from a clear set of stated rules and regulations. Instead, it draws upon the moral virtues of its people. Within those virtues, happiness does not come from independent financial success. To conduct healthy and beneficial business with the Chinese people, an awareness of virtues and rules of propriety is the starting point.

The quick overview of the two unique business contexts in the U.S. and China is meant to be a guide for thought and understanding and seeks to establish the importance of contextual understanding. The ample data collected in the study can be sliced and diced in countless ways to show differences between groups, but that is not the point of this book. As we journey further, chapter 3 takes you on an exploratory journey to look within first, and to discover the process of cultural exploration.

Closing food for thought: How can I refrain from making conclusive judgments about any group while maintaining openness for individual uniqueness?

Table 2.3.2. Success achievement comparison between generations.

Generation	Career Satisfaction	Happiness	Financial Success
1980s (18–29 years old)	4.27	**4.35**	3.96
1970s (30–39 years old)	4.51	**4.53**	4.04
1960s (40+ years old)	4.50	**4.72**	3.89

NOTES

1. Mengkui Wang, *China's Economy*, trans. Bengwen Lui (Beijing, China: China Intercontinental Press, 2004).
2. Jeanne Ellis Ormrod, *Educational Psychology: Developing Learners*, 5th ed. (Upper Saddle River, NJ: Pearson, 2006).
3. Ming-Jer Chen, *Inside Chinese Business: A Guide for Managers Worldwide* (Boston: Harvard Business Press, 2001).
4. Roy Jacques, *Manufacturing the Employee: Management Knowledge from the 19th to 21st Centuries* (Thousand Oaks, CA: Sage Publications, 1996).
5. Hay Group, "East Meets West: Bridging Two Great Business Cultures, March 2007," http://content.ll-0.com/haygroup1/east.pdf?i=062707122034 (accessed November 13, 2008).
6. Joanne B. Ciulla, *The Ethics of Leadership* (Belmont, CA: Thomson Wadsworth, 2003).

CHAPTER 3

MULTIDIMENSIONAL BUSINESS CONTEXTS

The complexity of business context offers countless opportunities for profits and knowledge acquisition. It is far more than the black-and-white simplicity that many theorists and behaviorists discuss in literature. Underneath the generalizations and categories, the human species has many dimensions of thought. Imagine the iceberg that sank the *Titanic*. You've placed enormous efforts and resources into making an idea come alive. After many months of planning and building, your idea now stands as a powerful *cruise ship*. As you sail onto the world economic ocean, it carries your life dreams, along with many others' hopes such as those of your employees and family. As you sail along, you see many other boats, large like the *Titanic* (major corporations) and small like a speedboat (entrepreneurial enterprises), trying hard to survive and dodge the many icebergs in a competitive environment. In your wisdom, you've hired an experienced captain who informs you of the many levels of complexity within the ocean, especially the complexity below the surface. As you view other boats sink, he tells you that sailing the economic ocean is not a simple one-dimensional game. Beneath the tip of each iceberg, there are many layers that can sink the most powerful of boats. Knowing what is beneath the iceberg is the fabric of sustainable success.

In Western business contexts, established laws often dictate the right and wrong of doing business. While the majority of the business is done through some form of a contract, established legal standards exist for every transaction. If you believe that, did you ever wonder why there is an abundance of lawyers in Western society? While there is an established duality—right and wrong—reality is often much more multifaceted. Regardless of the explicit laws that govern transactions, conflict and legal action are part of the business landscape.

The business context is much more complex than the explicit laws that attempt to regulate them. We do not live in a duality of right and wrong or black and white. Sustained profits go to those who operate in the middle, where multiplicity has balance.

Take for example the notions of individualism and collectivism. They are two opposite sides in a philosophy of life. On the surface, Americans accept the idea that we are an individualistic society. The basic operating unit is the individual.[1] We even have management theories that protect organizations from individualistic motivations, such as agency theory. According to this theory, people are driven by self-interest. As a result, they cannot be trusted to abide by the interests of the organization over personal interest. When a conflict of goals occurs, it is very difficult to assess whether the individual is making decisions in the best interest of the organization or his or herself.[2] Theories like this push people to look for self-motivated choices in everyday activities. Unfortunately, we only see the surface behaviors of individuals. With management training, people often resort to creating an individualized motivation without seeking further understanding. This practice is common even with the most educated executives and leaders. As a result, they end up blaming the individual with little or no responsibility for their role in a situation. They get to be "right" and others are "wrong." We are very good at finding what we focus on. And in this case, managers taught under agency theory focus on finding individualist motivations. In reality, they are only seeing the tip of the iceberg. There are numerous and unique influences for each individual beneath the visible behaviors.

Are Americans that simple to live within individualism? While this may be a huge philosophical debate, let's look at the data. Out of the 544 values selected in the study, family was the most often selected value. It also had the most points associated in order of importance. How does that align with the individualism assumption? If the culture was to be individualistic, participants would have selected individual values like personal achievement in their top eight. In reality, that value didn't make the top ten. It scored twelfth on the order of importance in the study. Family was the number one value. No other value received more than 10% of the points (family had 11.56%). Integrity was close at 8.21%. The rest of the values were around 5% of the total. Out of the top eight values, five of the eight were relational values like family, integrity, honesty, trust, and respect. These values call for a relationship to other people. Could the assumption of individualism be false? In another major study with nearly 2,000 business leaders across the world, one of the key measures was loyalty to community. The researchers also had a similar assumption that Americans and Canadians would score in the lowest group of ten countries across the world. Their data analysis proved this assumption to be false. Both Americans and Canadians were in the middle of the score range, not at the lowest score range.[3] This data further refutes the individualism assumption of Americans.

The Chinese are supposed to be a collectivist culture. Looking at the data from the Chinese business leaders, personal achievement scored as the number four priority. This individualistic value had a much higher position with the Chinese group than with the American group. Looking at the list of top eight values, more individualistic values appeared in the Chinese data. Values like career, competence and competition did not appear in the American data set. How could this be representative of a collectivist culture?

The answer is not that simple. The data is only one dimension of humanity. Values have significant influence on behaviors and decisions, but they are not the only drivers. Generalizations about a culture reduce the opportunities stemming from the many layers for discovery at the individual, group and organizational levels. When assuming that people are acting out of individualistic motivations, you may be missing out on crucial information that leads towards a healthy relationship without blind blame.

Dimensions of Business Leaders

When looking at the context of business, the individual is the basic element. Starting a business venture in any industry requires individuals to work together. Even with large corporations, the individual leaders who create trusting relationships enable profitable transactions. I've often found it fascinating to hear people talk about how an organization didn't treat them well or how their country raised import taxes and harmed the business. While it's easy to blame an entity, it also reduces one's ability to influence change. Whether it's an organization or a country, there are people working within the system who make decisions. While rules and policies guide people's decisions and behaviors, the individual involved always has many choices to treat you as a fellow human being. This is the empowered mentality of entrepreneurs who never let some artificial rule block their way. Instead, they work with others to overcome barriers.

■ MIND GEM 3.1 ■

Mind Gem 3.1: Making assumptions in business opens the door for significant risk and loss of opportunities. Most managers tend to assume the worst based on management paradigms like agency theory. They often assume that people are individualist in nature and will make decisions to enhance personal goals over organizational goals. As managers see one behavior, assumptions concerning an individualistic intent drive managers to create more rules for conformity without understanding the underlying thought process behind the behavior. Is it really necessary to create assumptions at all when you see a negative behavior? What if you refrained from such assumptions and kept an open mind? Here are a few steps to find the brilliance in humanity.

Tactical steps:

When you see an emotionally charged behavior (something that gets you fired up based on previous experiences such as business not being done at all during a meeting) . . .

1. Observe your mind's natural tendency to create "rational" explanations for another

continued on page 52

continued from page 51

person's behaviors. This could be either a negative (individualistic motivations) or a positive (for the good of the group) perspective.

2. Challenge your mind to think about the rationale with the opposite focus. If you felt that the behavior was to advance one's personal gain, focus on collective gain such as that of the company or a family. In other words, place the individual in a positive light if you initially had a negative assumption. This will illustrate your brain's ability to create reasons in both directions. Through this conscious role play, you may get into a confused state—which is a great state for learning. For example, you are attending a business meeting off site. While the meeting was scheduled to be one hour, you find yourself talking about everything else but the business topic for over an hour. An obvious assumption could be that the other party does not care about what is important to you. Now taking the opposite focus, what perfectly justified reasons exist? The other side could be more concerned with their own personal challenges within

continued on page 53

Within the context of international business, working with Chinese business leaders or companies involves relationships with individuals. By understanding the contextual web of interconnectedness within individual relationships, business leaders may seize many opportunities.

THE INIMITABLE ICEBERG

To successfully navigate your *Titanic* of valuable goods and services across the global economic ocean, knowing the makeup of individuals involved helps develop effective relationships. The *Inimitable Iceberg* represents a visual layout that combines many theories from psychology and business. Figure 3.1 illustrates the five levels of the iceberg. While reality is much more complex than a two dimensional figure can ever depict, this is one attempt at helping you navigate the depths of the global economic ocean. A mastery of understanding each individual's *Inimitable Iceberg* yields peaceful, balanced and powerful business leaders. From the surface, these leaders appear to always be in the right place at the right time. Doors automatically open for them to move products and services across cultural boundaries.

LEVEL 1: ABOVE THE WATERLINE

Thanks to the strategic choices and timing of B. F. Skinner, behaviorism dominates a significant portion of Western business thought. When you look at most books on leadership, they typically tell you about all the "right" behaviors of successful leaders. There are countless biographies of successful business leaders sharing their experiences and recommending behaviors. Some of the most

Figure 3.1. The *Inimitable Iceberg* depicts the many levels of complexity of a human being. While most people operate at the surface, working in behaviors and measuring performance, very few have the wisdom to dig beneath the surface towards the values/beliefs and identity level.

popular, like Collins' *Good to Great*, offers an abundance of behavioral tactics for effective leadership, such as "confronting the brutal facts."[4]

At the organizational level, many organizations measure activities and performance. It's always amazing for companies to find out that, at the end of the quarter, revenues won't meet projections. Often, it is too late to know when performance numbers won't make the mark. And whether they make the mark or not, what did they do right or wrong? What was the specific behavior at the individual and group systems that enabled and disabled success?

continued from page 52

the family. Or they could also be interested in you as a human being and not just as a medium for the business transaction—something foreign in most Western business contexts. Keeping an open mind, you will find many other possibilities exist.

continued on page 54

continued from page 53

3. In the midst of this state, ask the individual for their rationale/motivation. Start with the phrase "Help me understand your rationale for . . ." Be careful with word selection. The word "why" can be perceived as confrontational, as in "Why did you do this?" You want to make sure your mental framework is open with no attachment to a response. You may even tilt your head slightly to illustrate curiosity from a body language perspective.

Working on an international business level requires this basic skill. People from different cultures and regions may have completely different thought processes from your experiences. Getting into a habit of not forming blind assumptions based on your perceptions and seeking understanding helps you learn. More importantly, when you create genuine curiosity about an individual, the context of the question makes a clear message—I care about you; I value your ideas. Relationally, whether in the United States, China, or Austria, human beings embrace this contextual message when it is authentically delivered.

The majority of people live within behaviorism. It is a fun world where there's always a new behavior for any given situation. The possibilities are endless. I've often wondered if this is the root cause for the high divorce rates in many Western nations. Many people connect at the surface of behaviors and they share common activities. While this is a starting point for relationships, the rationale for engaging in the activity can be drastically different. One person may enjoy it for the competitive nature of an activity; another may enjoy it for the social aspect. And, as we age and develop, our interests change along with activities. If people connect only at the activity/behavior level, the changes of activities would result in a lack of common interests. Would this lead towards the big D?

In the business world, there are countless "proper" behaviors in business etiquette, business transactions, and business relationships. Within the hundreds of proper behaviors or traits, studies show that none have proven to yield effective leadership.[5] So why the huge focus on behaviors? It only confuses people from their own personality. The next time someone tells you to adopt a behavior, see if it is congruent with who you are first.

LEVEL 2: SKILLS DEVELOPMENT

Below the waterline is the skills level. This level represents the many abilities and experiences people gain in their lifetime. Some skills are relatively new, like using a pair of chopsticks at dinner. Others are well tuned, like making presentations. Skills are also neutral. For example, the ability to network at a gathering by passing out many business cards could be positive in Western society under some circumstances. In Eastern culture, network skills like this could be offensive, since relationships call for quality, not quantity. The conscious and wise application of skills calls for a high level of awareness in knowledge.

LEVEL 3: KNOWLEDGE

Do you know what you don't know that you don't know? This is a confusing statement to read. In other words, what don't you know about issues that are not in your awareness at all? When it comes of failure, it is often what we didn't know that influenced the failure. In organizational change literature, it's often the unknown that promotes fear and anxiety. Knowledge is a crucial aspect to humanity. Many theorists have stated that we're in a knowledge economy. While the past was driven by the muscles of laborers, today's competitive environment calls for knowledge workers.[6,7,8] The organizational context of learning becomes crucial since knowledge is often contained in individuals. The challenge of making tacit knowledge explicit became a focus for leaders.[8,9]

The one question inspired by Heidegger when it comes to knowledge is: How do you know if what you know is the truth, especially when it comes to a different culture?[10] Understanding that you don't know everything enables leaders to build effective relationships. It also calls for great humility to balance one's ego. One of the foundational principles of life shared by the Chinese is humility. Regardless of how much experience one may have or degrees one may possess, there is always ample room for learning.

Going back to the equation for learning presented in Chapter 2-1 (Information + Emotional attachment = Profound Knowledge), ego and humility are crucial aspects of that emotional attachment.[11] Individuals with ample ego have an emotional barrier to learning. This brings us to a connector that enables the learning of new knowledge and the shaping of values and beliefs—emotions. Emotions are like the thread that connects values and beliefs to knowledge. They can also be the enabler that shapes values and beliefs. Emotional intelligence is like a sphere that surrounds knowledge, values, and beliefs. It is like the road that enables the travels of information. Emotions are a primary source of power and influence within any system of people.[11]

LEVEL 4: VALUES AND BELIEFS

Values and beliefs are a steady aspect of who we are as an individual. They drive what we care about. When we have the courage to reach for a challenging goal, it is the belief that we can achieve it that leads the way. This level within the iceberg is the core of our makeup. From birth to your current age, values and beliefs are shaped by your many experiences and lessons. To understand the individuals operating in the global business context, values, and beliefs create the door to success. Before venturing out to explore others, knowledge of your own values and beliefs comes first. From Western philosophy, there is a movement to self-knowledge. Some leadership texts are beginning to explore the notion of self-knowledge before taking on external practices.[12] From Eastern philosophy, knowledge of self is also the starting point to knowledge of relationships with others.

LEVEL 5: IDENTITY

Identity is often mixed with roles, titles, or positions. In Western societies, people's professions may become their identity. We all have preconceived notions or images about what an accountant is like or how an engineer is supposed to think. In Chinese culture, hierarchies are important. Titles and positions accompany a person's achievement to a specific level of authority. The exciting exploration of identities starts with the realization that a human being is not stuck with any single identity. At any given time, one can choose to think differently, act innovatively, and respond strategically. There are countless roles and positions in the mix throughout an individual's lifetime. The exploration of identities will be very limited in this book, due to its psychological complexity. For the purpose of this book, the identity you'll learn to embody is that of an empowered leader.

A Values Discovery Process: Understanding the Individual Context

The majority of our cultural exploration journey starts at level four—values and beliefs. The following is a simple four-step process where you'll learn to define personal tacit values and create congruence between values and behavior. This creates an incredible level of awareness that promotes higher critical thought. In the journey of developing an increased awareness of values, you'll also be developing the crucial skills to learn about others' value systems. Once both sides have a clear understanding of each other's value systems and how they align, we'll then weave the powerful working relationship with the threads of values.

Each step of the values discovery process is an interactive process, requiring action on your part. The experiences and discoveries in this process are rather profound. I've had a chance to facilitate many of these discovery sessions with leaders from around the world. Every experience has taught me something new about specific individuals in specific cultures. Even when two people are from the same street in the same city, their values will differ, which drives many decisions and behaviors.

STEP 1: DEFINE TACIT VALUES

Individual values represent the desired mode of conduct or outcome.[13] Values represent what is important to an individual.[14] Each individual has a set of values called the values system. A systematic method for understanding one's self from an internal perspective is a necessary step for inner peace. The other side of inner peace is dealing with the increasing workplace stress that many leaders face. A smart leader desiring sustainable success would start with understanding his or her individual values system, since it highly influences individual behaviors.[14,15] The goal of this step is to create a high level of awareness of one's values system.

1. Start with writing down your top fifteen personal values. In writing, briefly define the values.
   a. Be sure that the words are single word values and not actions. For example, "providing quality customer service"—providing is an action driven by a value, not a value in itself. Another common myth is "communication." A skill is not a value; people communicate for various reasons. Respect may be an underlying value that drives people to communicate.
   b. You may also ask—is this for a family or professional setting? This is one of the many myths of management. The human being is not like a machine that can accurately and consistently separate two mental thought processes. If you attempt to do so, the lesser used process will be lost. We are an integrated whole. If you like, you're more than welcome to do this twice, one for family context and one for work. See how similar they are?
2. Reduce the values to top eight based on your priorities.
3. Then reduce it to your top five values.

STEP 2: CREATE INDIVIDUAL CONGRUENCE

Individual congruence describes the decision process that a person takes to merge their values and respective action within a specific situation.[16] The purpose of this step is to create an integrated self that is fully aware of his/her values system with every decision. During this step, the initial self-analysis intends to reveal individual inconsistencies between one's values system and behaviors. Although this is a difficult and perhaps even painful process, the lack of congruence stimulates learning and the desire to change.[11,14]

1. Over a three-day period, take 15-30 minute snapshots of your activity throughout the day. These snapshots include the type of activity and the decisions made during that engagement. At the end of three days, you will have a list of activities to reflect upon.

2. Make a photocopy of the list. We'll take two approaches for analysis.

a. Using this list, your analysis starts with clustering similar activities together. Then calculate the number of hours you spend on specific activities. Compare the time spent on specific activities and your top five values. How do they match? For example, one executive at a major global fashion company found that she spent on average 36 hours working on business issues, while only 9.5 hours on personal/family time over three days. This revealed an obvious incongruence, as this executive had listed family as one of her top values. The time difference between work and family illustrates an alternate value in opposition with the value of family.

b. With the other copy of the list, review the decisions made in the three-day period. Select a few memorable decisions and see if they align with your top values. For example, an international business networker decided to miss part of his son's afternoon soccer game so that he could finish working on a business proposal. When he reviewed the decision, he felt horrible knowing that he could have made the game and finished the proposal later that night. Many of us get caught up in attempting to finish an emotionless task; whether it's our ego or a need for accomplishment, this decision often causes lateness in meetings with friends and family. Think back to how many times you may have apologized for being late because "work" held you up.

A natural tendency during this step is to "fix" the incongruence. On the contrary, the goal here is *to simply understand the system, not attempt to fix it.* As the awareness of daily decisions and behaviors measured against one's values system increases, your thought process will automatically shift the behavior.

Before moving onto the next step, having personal experience of the process maintains the line for integrity. I have seen many workshop leaders cower in shame when they could not quickly share their values systems and personal journey towards congruence. Your personal efforts will also help you create a sense of understanding and empathy for others in the process.

STEP 3: SEEK VALUES OF OTHERS

Understanding the values of others around you seeks a deeper understanding between people with minimal time investment. Rather than the typical "what do you like to do in your free time" conversations, these conversations move directly toward core values. Before moving into step three, consider a quick *self-analysis* of beliefs by answering the following questions:

- Who am I within the context of this conversation?
- What are my beliefs about people working with me?
- What are my beliefs concerning the relationship with others (collaborative, hierarchical, etc.)?

How can a unique relationship be defined based on knowledge of individual values?

1. Adding the characteristics of *curiosity* and *fun* into this process, select two different people who know you well. Ideally, one should be a peer, while another can be a family member.
2. On a blank sheet of paper, write down what you believe to be their top five values. At the same time, ask them to write down what they believe to be your top five values.
3. Taking turns, each individual reveals their educated guess of the other's top five values. See how accurate you are in this process? A dialogue may likely occur over the next five to ten minutes to discuss actual and perceived values.

This process of understanding provides room for an individual at any level of the organization to learn about the values of individuals involved in business decisions. Such a dialogue facilitates reconciliation and clarification of myths between individuals from different cultural backgrounds. If you are working within a team structure, conduct this process within the team first. When you begin to work with a Chinese business group, conduct a similar process to see how the two cultures perceive each other after working with them for a few days.

STEP 4: CREATE A COLLABORATIVE VALUES SYSTEM

Steps one through three create the environment for understanding between Chinese and American business leaders. The collective values of all individuals form the collaborative values system. A simple *multi-voting process* solidifies the values system of the group. The process also calls for fairness, as every individual has equal weight in the multi-voting process.

1. List the individual values on a white board.
2. Each individual gets to have five votes. For simplicity, look at it as five sticky notes.
3. Have everyone walk up to the board and place their sticky notes as votes next to the value they see as a priority. One can either place all five votes on one value, or evenly distribute them across five values.

4. Total the points up and you will arrive at a values system with a specific priority for each value. You'll see a natural break point where votes are minimal. Typically, values with one or two votes do not make it onto the group values system.

Depending on the diversity of the group, you may find a larger set of values (above 10). In my experiences with conducting these processes, the most healthy and productive teams typically have around five to seven values that receive the majority of the votes. A lower number within the core values-set offers a more significant congruence between team members. A higher number within the values-set offers a greater diversity of perspectives.

This relational values system is a *living entity*. Many clients have adopted a practice of sharing and aligning values systems at an initial meeting for partnership or alliances. Before any discussions on business occur, leaders share and agree on the values that form the business context of the relationship. With a clear guidance, either side is responsible to maintain alignment of behaviors and the established values system. This process is one method for consciously creating a business context that translates into many decisions and behaviors above the surface.

NOTES

1. Ming-Jer Chen, *Inside Chinese Business: A Guide for Managers Worldwide* (Boston: Harvard Business Press, 2001).
2. Sumantra Ghoshal, "Bad Management Theories Are Destroying Good Management Practices," *Academy of Management Learning & Education*, 4(1) (March 2005): 75–91.
3. Zeynep Aycan, Rabindra N. Kanungo, Manuel Mendonca, Kaicheng Yu, Jurgen Deller, Gunter Stahl and Anwar Kurshid, "Impact of Culture on Human Resource Management Practices: A 10-Country Comparison," *Applied Psychology: An International Review*, 49(1) (January 2000): 192.
4. Jim C. Collins, *Good to Great: Why Some Companies Make the Leap . . . And Others Don't* (New York: Harper Collins, 2001).
5. Bernard M. Bass, *Bass & Stogdill's Handbook of Leadership*, 3rd ed. (New York: Free Press, 1990).
6. Peter F. Drucker, *Post-Capitalist Society* (Oxford: Butterworth Heonemann, 1993).
7. Roy Jacques, *Manufacturing the Employee: Management Knowledge from the 19th to 21st Centuries* (Thousand Oaks, CA: Sage Publications 1996).
8. Peter M. Senge, *The Fifth Discipline: The Age and Practice of the Learning Organization* (London: Century Business, 1990).
9. Ted Sun, *Survival Tactics: Top 11 Behaviors of Successful Entrepreneurs* (Westport, CT: Greenwood Publishing Group, 2007).

10. David F. Krell, ed., *Martin Heidegger Basic Writings: From Being and Time (1927) to The Task of Thinking (1964)* (New York: HarperCollins, 1993).

11. Robert K. Cooper and Aman Sawaf, *Executive EQ: Emotional intelligence in Business* (Berkeley, CA: Berkeley Publishing Group, 1998).

12. James G. Clawson, *Level Three Leadership: Getting Below the Surface*, 3rd ed. (New York: Pearson, 2006).

13. Milton Rokeach, *The Nature of Human Values* (New York: Free Press, 1973).

14. Steve Bavister and Amanda Vickers, *Teach Yourself NLP* (Chicago: Contemporary Books, 2004).

15. Stephen P. Robbins, *Essentials of Organizational Behavior* (Upper Saddle River, NJ: Prentice Hall, 2005).

16. Lloyd C. Williams, *The Congruence of People and Organizations: Healing Dysfunction from the Inside Out* (Westport, CT: Quorum Books, 1993).

WESTERN BELIEFS AND VALUES

We conducted a study that looked at the values system and a small set of beliefs within the Western business community (mainly the United States and some data from European nations). While it would be ideal to gather data from many more developed nations, access to the various populations is rather challenging. Even within the United States, asking people to participate in a study is tough with the limited free time that haunts the population. The depth of thought required by the survey instrument makes this participation more challenging. One friend, who is also a professor at Pace University, commented after taking the survey, "Very interesting and very difficult!"

To maximize data collection, the study broke the instrument into three sections. They are 1) Value ranking; 2) Values congruence; 3) Beliefs congruence. At each section of the study, the participant may stop at any point while still contributing to the previous section independently. This design consideration allowed busy professionals to only contribute to the initial ranking of values, without getting into the details of values and beliefs congruence sections.

The resulting data from the Western business community is from 98 business leaders. The majority of the participants were executive-level leaders in various organizations. 90.8% possessed a university degree with 39.8% possessing a masters or a doctorate degree. The participants were from many states in the United States, including New York, Connecticut, Ohio, Arkansas, Texas, Florida, and many more. While a number of leaders participated in the study from European nations such as the United Kingdom, Switzerland, and Germany, they did not have significant numbers to accurately define a separate population. The results presented going forward are mostly driven by American participants as one representation of Western business context. While one could argue the statistical significance of this representation, there is no doubt that the American economy and its business practices have a significant influence in the global context of business. Starting in the second half of 2008, the economic crisis experienced by the world is direct proof of this influence. The following presents a high-level overview of the analysis.

Top Values

As mentioned previously, values and beliefs significantly influence the way we think.[1,2] Before working with other cultures, especially the Chinese who greatly value self-knowledge and relationships, understanding your personal and cultural value system is a crucial starting point.[3]

Many cultures, including Westerners, believe that Western society (like the United States and Canada) is primarily individualistic.[4] Many theories have the fundamental assumption that when given the chance, people will act out of their own personal interest. Significant management thought also shares these assumptions. They assume that the average worker is child-like and needs to be guided within a clear hierarchical structure. Furthermore, many practices continue to limit decisions from the top, which assumes employees' lack of ability to be creative and to make unselfish decisions.[5]

On the contrary, the study illustrated clear evidence against individualism. Out of a comprehensive list of 63 values, family was the dominant value, especially as the most frequently selected top value (see figure 3.1.1). The value of family covered 32.35% of all selections as the choice for the top value.

Two statistical methods of analysis illustrate similar results. The first method used a point rating process. Each value selected in the study received

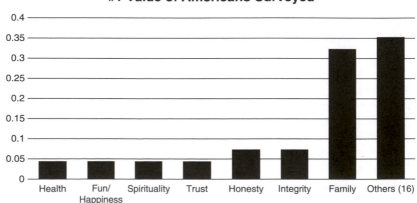

Figure 3.1.1. The frequency of values selected as the most important value.

specific points based on the priority. If a value was the top priority, it received eight points. The second priority value received seven points. Totaling all of the points together, the results reveal a values system of eight values (see table 3.1-1). Family was by far the most dominant from the study at 11.56%.

The second method used to evaluate order of value importance was frequency analysis. In this approach, the higher frequency illustrates the number of times participants selected a specific value. Table 3.1-2 illustrates the top eight values according to this analysis method. The two methods both agree that family and integrity are the most important values.

The total percentage at the bottom of tables 3.1-1 and 3.1-2 provide an insight on the homogeneity of the population. Higher values of total percentage would indicate a population that is very similar in core values. Lower total percentage of the top eight would indicate diversity within the population. If you were to take a guess, how would you rate the diversity of values

Table 3.1-1. Top eight values by total points (n = 73).

	Values	Point Rating
1.	Family	11.56%
2.	Integrity	8.21%
3.	Honesty	5.51%
4.	Health	4.98%
5.	Fun/Happiness	4.86%
6.	Passion	4.13%
7.	Trust	3.72%
8.	Respect	3.39%
	Total	46.36%

Table 3.1-2. Top eight values selected by frequency in the top eight (out of 759 selections).

	Values	Selection Frequency
1.	Family	7.77%
2.	Integrity	6.72%
3.	Fun/Happiness	4.48%
4.	Passion	4.22%
5.	Honesty	4.08%
6.	Health	3.69%
7.	Trust	3.56%
8.	Respect	3.29%
	Total	37.81%

in China compared to those of Western cultures as in the United States? Jot this down and find the answers in chapter 3.4.

Another dimension of values looked to quantify the concept of family, since people have more than one definition of family. The highest level of importance found in the study was the ability to spend time with family and the closeness of relationships. Unfortunately, the ability to behave according to these values was relatively low. As defined in chapter 2.2, congruence is one's ability to behave according to one's values system. If an individual is highly congruent, they are able to behave according to their values most of the time. This would yield a near 100%. However, life is not that simple. The complexity of the global business environment and the mixture of intra-personal values do not allow any individual to live at 100% congruence. As a result, the highest level of congruence established was 90.1% from the Chinese data analysis and 80.89% from the Western data analysis.

With respect to the top value of family, congruence of the amount of time spent with family with that desired is only 57.83%. This measure of congruence reflects the challenges of work-life balance. While most people would like to spend more time with family and value it as their top priority, they are not able to achieve it. Combining the five different perspectives on family, the study found an overall congruence to family of 64.88% (see table 3.1-3).

The second most important value was integrity. Three different measures of integrity all yielded a high level of importance (range of 4.92 to 5.15 out of 6). The study looked at integrity from three different perspectives. The first is about being able to follow through with promises. The second is the honor of one's words. The last is one's integrity to self. It is the choice to always stand up for one's beliefs. When looking at the congruence values (see table 3.1-4), the one that stands out is the honor of one's word. While it possessed a similar level of importance, most people within the study were not congruent. This also led to a lower level of congruence overall with a 47.71% on integrity.

Table 3.1-3. Congruence measures to family.

Overall Congruence	Family Time	Closeness of Relationships	Purpose for Work	Purpose for Achievement	Family Pride
64.88%	57.83%	60.91%	67.88%	67.60%	70.20%

Table 3.1-4. Congruence measures to integrity.

Overall Congruence	Promise Follow-through	Honor of One's Word	Self Integrity
47.71%	53.45%	35.21%	54.48%

The results portray accurate reflections of challenges within Western society. The increasing demands of a global economy drive people to work harder. As a result, work-life balance is a major challenge, with more and more people spending the majority of their waking hours working. Especially with technology, businesses have a constant leash on their employees. The challenge of integrity at near 50% reflects the overwhelming pressures exerted by business environments on individuals. While many see it as an important attribute, few are able to consistently maintain their integrity.

Value Systems Uniqueness

From an international perspective, many countries tend to generalize what it means to be an American. As they think of other relatively foreign cultures, many Americans tend to think the Chinese people are one single homogenous group. Both assumptions are far from the truth. Since America is a melting pot, values are not consistent across the entire country. We took a quick look at how different values and their respective congruence may be between geographic regions and genders. The results are rather interesting.

VALUES COMPARISON

Table 3.1-5 illustrates the differences between data from a few Northeast coast states and the Midwest. I had a special interest in these two regions, since I grew up in New York City and lived most of my adult life in the Midwest. From my personal experiences, there are significant differences between the two regions. According to the data, family, health, and integrity were relatively consistent, with a high degree of importance to both regions. The value of honesty is extremely interesting. Having lived in a major East Coast city like New York, people are much more up front with you, since they have no time to play games. People in New York "tell it like it is" for the most part. Living in the Midwest (Columbus, Ohio), many people are very concerned with the emotions of others. Honesty has to have a balance

Table 3.1-5. Value systems comparison by geographic regions.

Priority	East Coast (NY, NH, CT)	Midwest Values (OH, IN)
1.	Family	Family
2.	Health	Integrity
3.	Integrity	*Honesty*
4.	*Passion*	Health
5.	*Respect*	*Freedom*
6.	Spirituality	*Religion*
7.	Trust	Spirituality
8.	Fairness	Trust

with the perception of hurt feelings. In the hundreds of workshops I've conducted in the Midwest, honesty is usually a topic of discussion when it comes to values. The majority of attendees at every workshop would state their desire to be 100 percent honest, but they would also admit that it is not possible. Different people have varying degrees of consideration for another's feelings.

Another major difference between the two regions is reflected in spirituality and religion. It was quite ironic for both to show up as number six in the priority of values. While the East Coast region only had spirituality in the top eight, the Midwest had both religion and spirituality. This evidence illustrates the conservative nature of the Midwest. In my personal experiences, people on the East Coast, which has more dense population centers compared to the Midwest, have a higher sense of self-efficacy as individuals. People in the Midwest focus more on the group experience with the higher power.

Both values of spirituality/religion and honesty have significant influence when working with the Chinese. From an honesty perspective, honor and respect carry a heavy influence on the context of saving face. While many Chinese presume that Americans tend to be too honest and outspoken, visiting business leaders can be honest to a certain, modest degree. Applying the hurt feelings rationale of the Midwest may greatly benefit relationship building. If feelings are hurt and you disgrace a person of influence, your chances of success are virtually nonexistent. Speaking honestly may confirm the arrogance associated with Americans.

From a spirituality/religion perspective, can you guess which side of the coin the Chinese fall on? As we will discuss further in detail in chapter 3.4, the value of religion is not selected by any Chinese. Instead, the Chinese people focus on inner harmony.

Table 3.1-6 illustrates value differences between males and females. It's quite interesting to see the top values of family and integrity have different priorities within genders. While family is at the top of the female priority, integrity is the males' top priority. This might indicate some of the natural challenges that males and females have when it comes to relationships. On one hand, males valued leadership in their top eight values; females did not have

Table 3.1-6. Value systems comparison by gender.

Priority	Female Values	Male Values
1.	**Family**	**Integrity**
2.	**Integrity**	**Family**
3.	Fun/Happiness	Honesty
4.	Health	Fun/Happiness
5.	Passion	**Leadership**
6.	**Empathy/Kindness**	Passion
7.	Honesty	Respect
8.	**Financial Independence**	Trust

that in their list. On the other hand, females had empathy/kindness as well as financial independence in their list. One could expect females to have empathy due to a greater sense of emotional awareness. But the value of financial independence was a bit surprising, while it did not show up in the males' top eight values. This could be one rationale for the increasing amount of females in the workforce, seeking to gain their own financial independence.

VALUES CONGRUENCE COMPARISONS

The degree of congruence between the regions and the gender groups are also unique. Overall, the data analysis revealed a values congruence measure of 59.5%. This could be one of the many contributing factors to the major health issues that exist in most organizations. When people are not able to be or choose not to be congruent to their values system, the level of cognitive dissonance can cause significant stress. If unresolved, continued high levels of stress lead to many forms of illness, ranging from sleep disorders to depression.

Table 3.1-7 illustrates some differences in regional and gender congruence levels. The East Coast data vary greatly in congruence between the first and the second values, while the Midwest remained relatively steady across the top three values. In the gender comparisons, it's very interesting to see the significant difference in congruence. Males in the study had much higher congruence to values compared to females on all three top values.

While the results above provide a high level perspective of values in the Western business context, the unique results in gender and region exemplify the clear need to seek understanding of an individual without making blind assumptions. There are many other ways we could have divided the data, such as by level of education and by age groups or generations; all would yield a similar degree of differences. Rather than employing simple generalizations or stereotypes, successful business leaders make the effort to discover the brilliance and beauty of humanity in each individual.

Table 3.1-7. Values congruence matrix by priority of value and regional/gender differences.

	1st Value Congruence	2nd Value Congruence	3rd Value Congruence
Midwest	58.15%	58.87%	66.78%
East Coast	**73.80%**	**50.03%**	79.33%
Females	**51.02%**	48.78%	56.05%
Males	**75.95%**	73.26%	74.08%

Belief Systems Uniqueness

Similar to values, beliefs also play a significant role in determining behaviors and thought processes.[1] Beliefs can limit one's potential or establish innovative thought. There are countless beliefs concerning objects, roles, concepts, and norms. No single instrument is capable of assessing all of the beliefs that may exist. From a scholarly perspective, people's beliefs are their epistemological foundation. Epistemology is the study of knowledge. For example, the word *love* or *business* has a set of basic assumptions based on individual experiences. Epistemology seeks to understand how we define love or business and how do we know if it is a *truth* shared by others. The basic set of questions exists around beliefs as they do around knowledge. How does one come to have a certain belief? How do you know if a belief is a truth or a myth? How can one justify belief in a diverse global environment? These questions help leaders maintain a high level of awareness while keeping humility close by.

In order to make the study reasonable and not too long, nine beliefs composed the belief assessment. The beliefs are listed in table 3.1-8. They each play a crucial role in business decisions, from relationships to organizational structure and design. Especially when considering Western and Chinese business practices, these beliefs may cause significant conflict if both sides are not aware of the different positions held by the other.

The data confirms some obvious beliefs held by Western cultures. Comparatively, individualism (4.21 out of 6) is rated higher than collectivism (3.53). The sense of equality drives power distance (3.65) relatively low. The highest scores were life purpose and self-efficacy. From a congruence perspective (see table 3.1-9), the lowest is relationships. While people in Western society believe in having effective relationships, they choose not to be congruent in many situations. Many may also feel that they do not possess the power to change an environment that causes harm in relationship over other items of value like money and position. Similar to the congruence of values (at 59.5%), congruence of beliefs were also in the fifty percentile range (54.1%).

From a regional and gender perspective, the levels of importance on beliefs did not differ as significantly as they did in the values comparisons. The largest difference in the degree of importance was self-efficacy. East Coast results (5.18) had a higher sense of self-efficacy than those from the Midwest (4.63). This could be related to lifestyle differences, as the competition in larger cities and the speed of the cities are greater in the East Coast cities than in the Midwest. The more interesting results came from the analysis of belief congruence. From a regional perspective, the East Coast results show much lower measures of congruence in self-efficacy, life purpose, individualism, and foreigner trust. Especially with self-efficacy, the East Coast had the lowest measure of congruence at 29.44% out of all the beliefs. The Midwest had the highest measure of congruence with self-efficacy at 70.29%. Similarly, gender differences also existed in each of the beliefs. Although not as drastic in differences, the females were about 10% lower in congruence with most beliefs.

Table 3.1-8. Brief description of beliefs in the study.

Belief	Description
Self-Efficacy	This belief focuses on one's self-image. People with high levels of self-efficacy have confidence, especially when working with unknown or constant changes. They are conscious of what is important and how to reach goals.
Life Purpose	Life purpose is a belief related to spirituality. Some cultures believe in a higher calling for their life, while others believe in one's own choices that define life.
Power Distance	Power distance defines the degree of hierarchy that's necessary for society to function. People with a high belief of power distance will easily conform to decisions made by executives with minimal question. Low power distances calls for a partnership context with a relatively flat structure.
Paternalism	Paternalism deals with one's belief concerning the role of employers or governments. High scores in paternalism would indicate a codependent relationship between the individual and the employer. (While this could also be also used to define family or community roles, we're keeping this within the business context.)
Collectivism	Collectivism is a belief that places the needs of the community above all other personal needs. The community may decide what the goals are and concern for relationships within the group becomes a primary influence for decisions.
Individualism	Individualism is one's focus on self-development and needs over those of the employer.
Proactivity	Proactivity is another dimension of individualism. It deals with one's belief about working on a task without input from others. There's a sense of self-empowerment for high scores in proactivity.
Relationships	Relationships represent one's focus on the relations between people. High scores in the belief in relationships will often supersede other business gains like profit. This is of special interest working with the Chinese, who define their individuality with relationships.[3]
Foreigners' Trust	This last belief is one element in relationships. The intent to include this belief illustrates the difficulty a foreign business may have when entering a new market.

Table 3.1-9. Beliefs congruence matrix by priority of value and regional/gender differences.

	Self Efficacy	Life Purpose	Power Distance	Paternalism	Collectivism	Individualism	Proactivity	Relationships	Foreigners' Trust
Belief Ratings	**4.84**	**4.95**	3.65	4.13	**3.53**	**4.21**	4.45	4.52	4.62
Congruence	63.03%	56.73%	60.97%	53.54%	62.15%	55.90%	44.55%	**36.10%**	53.58%

Table 3.1-10. Beliefs congruence grouped by region and gender.

	Self Efficacy	Life Purpose	Power Distance	Paternalism	Collectivism	Individualism	Proactivity	Relationships	Foreigners' Trust
East Coast	**29.44%**	**34.25%**	56.05%	54.36%	61.07%	**42.41%**	30.65%	42.17%	**36.67%**
Midwest	**70.29%**	**56.65%**	65.44%	57.60%	61.26%	**65.45%**	48.18%	43.61%	**52.15%**
Female	59.08%	53.47%	56.11%	54.74%	58.56%	50.34%	37.81%	43.44%	48.95%
Male	71.59%	66.40%	74.58%	67.70%	72.94%	71.91%	62.22%	53.04%	64.61%

Table 3.1-11. Overall averages of belief congruence grouped by region and gender.

Region/Gender	Congruence Measure
East Coast	43.01%
Midwest	57.85%
Female	51.39%
Male	67.22%

Putting these belief congruence measures together, it's obvious that the overall values differ from one region to another and between males and females. From a regional perspective, the Midwest results (57.85%) reveal a higher measure of congruence on beliefs compared to the East Coast results (43.01%). This result is opposite to the values congruence where the East Coast had greater results. From the gender perspective, the results are consistent with the values congruence as they both show that males are more congruent than females.

The results from the study illustrate the complexity of values and beliefs and its many dimensions of uniqueness from regions to genders. With each belief or value, many interpretations and connotations cloud the context. Even if two individuals share the same level of importance on a value or belief, their level of congruence may be drastically different depending on one's environment. The various dimensions of beliefs and values yield drastically different behaviors and decisions in any business context.

NOTES

1. Steve Bavister and Amanda Vickers, *Teach Yourself NLP* (Chicago: Contemporary Books, 2004).
2. Ted Sun, "Leading Sustainable Change through Self-Discovery" (paper presented at the United Nations Global Forum: Business as an Agent of World Benefit: Management Knowledge Leading Positive Change, Case Western Reserve University, January 4, 2007). http://www.executive-balance.com/UNLeadingSustainableChange.
3. Ming-Jer Chen, *Inside Chinese Business: A Guide for Managers Worldwide* (Boston: Harvard Business Press, 2001).
4. Zeynep Aycan, Rabindra N. Kanungo, Manuel Mendonca, Kaicheng Yu, Jurgen Deller, Gunter Stahl and Anwar Kurshid, "Impact of Culture on Human Resource Management Practices: A 10-Country Comparison." *Applied Psychology: An International Review*, 49(1) (January 2000), 192.
5. Roy Jacques, *Manufacturing the Employee: Management Knowledge from the 19th to 21st Centuries* (Thousand Oaks, CA: Sage Publications, 1996).

WESTERN BUSINESS PRINCIPLES AND THEIR CHALLENGES

Why do you think obesity is such a huge problem in Western societies such as the United States and the United Kingdom? Why are health costs such a major concern? What relationship do business principles have with these national epidemics? More importantly, would you carry a disease into another culture?

In our cultural exploration journey, knowing one's self and where you are is the starting point. While many may be aware of the surface-level issues, the systemic view is hidden from consciousness. The thoughts in this section offer incredible opportunities for leadership within most organizations. It can help you understand the systems that drive behaviors and decisions that lead to many diseases. That's the first benefit. The second benefit to developing this insight is respect. Consequentially, knowledge at the systemic level of business provides meaningful and wise dialogue with Chinese business leaders who value systemic insight from a philosophical and historical perspective. Looking at the foundations of the Chinese culture, philosophies like those of Confucius and Lao Tzu play a crucial role in thought processes. Conversations at this level earn you the respect of Chinese leaders.

Discontinuous Change and Out-of-Date Business Principles

The business world of today is drastically different from the Industrial Revolution that initiated many management principles. As early as the mid-1990s, theories have commented on the unprecedented amount of change that is often traumatic in a global economy.[1,2] Today, the massive changes in large and complex organizations are more frequent than ever. Many *Fortune 100* companies strive to reinvent themselves in order to maintain a competitive advantage. Especially with globalization, many organizations such as Sun Microsystems and Conoco Phillips employ people from numerous ethnic and cultural foundations. This diverse workforce further complicates organizational change issues.[3] In addition, the increase in technological advances further challenges people at all levels of organizations. Especially with organizations' hierarchical decisions on technology infrastructure, the levels of stress when adopting new technologies further complicate the employees' perception of numerous organizational changes.[4] These environmental forces drive organizational change to be discontinuous, traumatic, and constantly increasing.

Unfortunately, all of these changes require new theories and models of business. The increasing health care issues and workplace stress, along with a limited level of innovation, are merely signs of an aging system unfit for today's environment. The conventional principles of how businesses function instigate many challenges in management practices, the legal environment, use of avoidant norms like blame and judgment, and a slow transition to a knowledge economy; they are like a disease, eating its way from the inside out. The lack of full understanding of these challenges further complicates any international ventures. Like a contagious virus, conventional principles would spread to another country with little or no immunity to the virus. As history has shown, the early explorers of the European empires in the 1600s and 1700s killed significant populations, not with their advanced technology, but with their diseases.[5] While the business viruses may not be as efficient as the 17th and 18th century disease carriers, their deadly effects can greatly harm another society. The major issues of developed Western nations such as obesity, a high percentage of the population on drugs for basic survival, and high workplace stress continue to provide a symptomatic window to systemic issues in business. While conventional principles have enabled incredible growth during the Industrial Revolution, the current knowledge economy has little room for such illness. One could also correlate these issues towards the losing of the technology advantage by Western societies to Japan and Korea. In another example, while America is a dominant power in world economics, a report indicated over 11 million Americans experience pain as a significant disability. Many more take pain medication on a regular basis to yield an incredible pharmaceutical industry that only addresses the symptoms.[6] What are the root causes of such diseases?

Since most people spend the majority of their waking hours at work (more than any other single activity), conventional business principles have a significant influence on the well-being of society. In many organizations, the levels of toxicity in political and hierarchical practices cause significant cognitive dissonance. For example, how many people do you know are forced to do something they do not wish to do, but feel that they have to in order to keep their jobs? The Western world has popular songs like "Take This Job and Shove It." On one hand, the organization talks the new language of leadership such as empowerment and teamwork; on the other, changes and decisions are passed downwards from the top with conformity expectations. This leads to many issues like obesity. I often find it saddening to see people make such a great effort to lose weight with diet and exercise. Some even receive an enormous amount of education on proper nutrition. All of that knowledge has limited influence. At the end of the workday, the stress experienced in the long day at work does not inspire people to go home and cook a healthy meal. The increasing tasks loaded onto employees without consideration do not allow a person time to find a healthy lunch and eat slowly. One of the major challenges in society today is the reductionist approach where specializations only focus on the problem. In this case, the problem of obesity received attention at the physical level only (medication, diet, exercise). Reducing a problem to its simplest part does not allow the system of interconnected events to reveal the root cause. This is one of the major differences with the Chinese culture, which is built on the interconnectedness of relationships and histories. Business is not just business. It's a significant portion of life and has momentous influence on wellbeing.

Management Principles

Management theory is a major contributor to business principles. Before reaching a high-level position, most people work through the system and become experts within the existing system. At the same time, the system also programs people to focus only on performance. The scandals led by chief executive officers of companies like Enron and Tyco challenged the conventional ethical principles of business in the past decade.[7] Rather than blaming the individuals involved alone for these unethical fallouts, maybe we should blame the theorists. Theories of management created the business systems that precipitated these fallouts, after all. According to Clawson, a leading author of leadership, different people within the same system would likely produce similar results.[8] Other established experts also supported this concept with a call for business schools to stop teaching old management principles that are out-of-date and harmful to organizational systems.[9] A systemic approach empowers leaders to take a fresh look in their role within organizational systems without blaming individuals.[8,10]

The thought processes and beliefs of many people embed the principles of management that started during the Industrial Revolution.[8] For example, many organizations explicitly state their value of respect for their employees. At the same time, the majority of organizations function with a hierarchical structure. The structure forces decisions downward with minimal to no input from lower-level employees. As a result, decisions that impact people's lives have little authentic ownership. With this "normal structure/process" in mind, is there respect when people are being told what to do and how to do something? This is one of the reasons for the many change theories that attempt to deal with the surface level challenge of resistance to change.

HARMFUL HIERARCHIES

Unless you are the CEO of the company your entire life, you have probably experienced many occasions where the only choice you have is conformity to a decision concerning how and what to do. This is a result of the hierarchical structure of organizations that forces people into conformity. A brief overview of history provides the rationale for the dominance of this structure.

Before the Industrial Revolution, most organizations were small shops where people used the apprentice model to become their own entrepreneurs. When the Industrial Revolution arrived, capitalists realized the need for a significant workforce to operate the machines in assembly lines. The only existing model for large organizations at that time was the military. As a result, manufacturing companies borrowed the hierarchical structure from the military to control the large workforce. Within this structure, the officers (there's a reason why the top level officials in companies are all called officers—CEO, COO, CIO) maintained all decision-making authority. Workers' ideas were irrelevant, as the value of their role was only physical. This structure was very successful in controlling a large population of workers to exploit labor in the Industrial Revolution.[11]

As we have moved into the knowledge economy, the demands of the workforce have changed drastically. While global competition requires innovative ideas to fuel success, most of organizational structures remain the same, along with business education.[9] The vocational movement in the early 1900s created the educational system of explicit hierarchy. At a very young age, you've learned that your school grades often determine your worth as a child. How absurd does it sound when a single hierarchical figure determines your worth with a grade as early as elementary school? While school offers great knowledge, the one-dimensional determination of a person's worth eliminates a holistic perspective of your worth at a very young age. Even with many courses on leadership, which is only taught at the university levels, the context of a hierarchical structure force students to conform and listen to lectures. Hierarchical structures greatly limit the basic human need to be heard and minimize one's self worth, especially in a knowledge economy. So when people resist change imposed on them, the common management *blame* is that they are resistant people. Instead, the system of hierarchy creates these systemic problems.

Within the knowledge economy, knowledge does not have to exist in a hierarchy. Rather than hoarding information to maintain power, trusting the collective wisdom of the team yields all kinds of rewards. Some significant rewards include trust and respect from others in the relational perspective. This is especially crucial when working with Chinese business leaders. Decision making comes from all levels of the organization. Decision making is also not about the duality of success or failure, nor is it about winning. Decision making focuses on understanding the needs of the employees while unleashing the potentials of collective wisdom and growing that wisdom by learning together. If a decision yields an undesirable result, it is simply a great lesson for the team to learn. While the hierarchy still exists in transactional tasks, it does not restrict the knowledge dimension that's crucial for success.

Relating the systemic challenges in theory to our study on values and beliefs, structure was one of the values that was not chosen once out of 759 selections. It is fascinating to see the amount of hierarchical structures in organizations from government to businesses; on the contrary, the leaders in our study did not value structure. This brings us to an interesting question—while people do not value structure, are they aware of the rigid structure they work with everyday? The results in the belief of power distance were also consistent with the unimportance of structure. Participants felt that collaborating to make decisions (5.34 out of 6) is more important than obeying decisions from the top (3.66 out of 6). The lack of importance on the value of structure and the belief in collaboration illustrates a significant philosophical difference with management practices. Could this be one of the causes for workplace stress that haunts countless organizations?

Legal Environment

The Western business world is driven by a strong legal system built on the content of situations. Thousands of laws at regional, national, and international levels attempt to guide everyday interactions between organizations and their constituents/clients/customers. While the content system provides a peaceful mechanism to enforce contracts, it failed to prevent businesses from suing each other. According to Charlie Wilson, a tenured professor of law at The Ohio State University, businesses bring the overwhelming majority of civil lawsuits in the United States. Within this system, many legislators continue to enhance existing laws while creating new ones for new situations and technologies. At the same time, the interpretation of law and creation of contracts requires significant diligence. All of these activities occur within the context of a specific culture. Due to the content nature of regulations, many Western laws have a basic assumption about the culture of a developed nation. This becomes a significant issue when working with other cultures, especially those who have developing status.

For example, America has very clear laws about child labor and minimum wages. As a developed country, its past in the Industrial Revolution taught society many valuable lessons about working conditions. While America was on its path toward industrialization, child labor was common. A child could work between 12-14 hours on average, with lower pay than an adult. As much as 86% of workers in Britain were below the age of 14 in the early 1700s. Famous author Charles Dickens was forced to work at the age of 12. In 1840, only 20% of children had some sort of schooling (including as little as one day per week). Both the United States and United Kingdom (Britain in those days) exploited children as a workforce in the early years of the Industrial Revolution.[12] It took significant efforts by activists to create legal guidelines that improved the situation. During the same time, reforms in education also played a role for children as they now had an alternative activity besides work. While children of developed nations now enjoy the protection of law, the cheap labor force they originally populated had a role in moving these developed nations forward. As horrific as it may have been for children, developed nations also learned from this necessary step. Applying laws concerning child labor to other nations isn't as simple. Many countries do not have the infrastructure of schools and other organized developmental activities for children. Without work, these low-income families would face hardship beyond the imagination of developed countries. The lack of an educational system could lead the children into other activities such as gangs and mischief. The application of laws without contextual consideration may greatly limit the lessons that a nation needs to learn.

From a Western perspective, business relationships are also legal relationships. In any international business venture, many considerations are necessary, such as the choice-of-law provision which specifies the legal framework for the contract.[13] As you approach the legal aspect of international business with the Chinese, be very careful with blind application of the Western business perspective. Many of the laws that appear to be reasonable in a developed nation may not apply in developing countries. Especially when the income disparities are drastic, a government's first goal is to create stability in the region, not to comply with some foreign law that has no consideration of the cultural context. Learning to balance the laws that guide your behaviors in the eyes of a Western culture and the accepted norms of a developing country with a drastically different historical path will be an ultimate test of a leader.

Avoidant Norms

Avoidant norms include two thought processes—judgment and blame. Beneath the thought processes, categorization is a "normal" practice of Western businesses. This stems from a dominant reductionist approach to life that attempts to place everything and all people into specific categories. So when you see someone behaving in a certain way, it's normal to place a generalized label on that individual. While it has its place in mechanistic processes of machines, the application on human beings causes huge challenges.

The fundamentals of reductionism look at the parts that make up the whole, without careful consideration of the relationships between the parts. From a mechanical perspective, $1 + 1$ will always equal 2. Or a car will always have wheels and an engine. Reductionists group people into categories, such as a Myers-Briggs personality type. If an individual is considered an extravert, that person is fit for specific jobs that involve working with people. There are two fundamental challenges with this approach. First, a person's preference to be an extravert does not provide insight on when he/she will be an introvert. As human beings, there are always environmental considerations that lead towards being an introvert over an extravert. We have the freedom of choice to be either at any time. The second challenge is the duality. While a square peg will always be a square peg, how many preferences can a person have? Do we really live in either one state or another state? Can't we live in both states at the same time in the same interaction? I've always found the popularity of the Myers-Briggs personality type fascinating, especially considering the lack of statistical validity in the instrument. It's also popular because of its simplicity. It's much easier to manage people when you assume a simple duality. Yet, no one wants to be categorized and fixed as a single characteristic.

Another word for categorization is stereotyping. Of course this term has negative connotations that business experts challenge people to avoid. But isn't the practice of categorization the same as the practice of stereotyping people? One may be by personality or job title, the other by color or ethnic background. We've all been well educated to know the answer to the following question—what happens when you stereotype people? Yet, we live in a world where categorization dominates organizations. We've all heard managers talk about the "lazy" or "unproductive" employees and what to do with them. One of the major challenges with categorization is blame. When managers categorize people into a negative group, they relinquish any power of influence or responsibility. The category provides managers a general intervention to fix the "problem." In fact, the problem may be the managers themselves or a system that does not understand the motivations of its people.

Human beings aren't that simple. We have unlimited potential from our creativity and emotional drive. Just think back to the days of your last vacation. How much more work were you able to accomplish the day or two before departing? 200 percent? 300 percent? As knowledge workers, this is far from a simple linear equation. The innovation that the human mind creates from passion and emotional focus allows us to increase productivity exponentially by choice. The passion and drive for the vacation may have provided the focus you needed to accomplish

■ MIND GEM 3.2 ■

Mind Gem 3.2: What boxes contain me? What categorizations have I allowed others to label me with? Many people have mental prisons that restrict their potential. While some societies live on the principle that you can become anyone you choose in theory, the containers of human existence are everywhere. The historical achievement of Obama's presidential election provides a great example of the possibilities. So let's explore your containers of thought with the goal of increased awareness. In that awareness, you have the empowered choice to be in an "unbounded space of thought."

Tactical steps:

Find yourself a quiet place and answer the following questions in writing:

1. Who am I? List the answers on a piece of paper.
2. Can I be more than one role at a time without violating the space of the other? Match up a few of the roles you have defined.
3. What are some characteristics, skills, and abilities associated with those roles listed?

continued on page 82

continued from page 81

4. How are these characteristics, skills, and abilities represented in me?
5. Can I maintain all of these characteristics, skills, and abilities?
6. What other roles can I take with these characteristics, skills, and abilities?
7. Who am I?

This exercise does not have examples, in order for you to interpret the questions as you see fit. This may be a challenging exploration to expand your view of self. Once you have a higher level of awareness, review the labels you place on others. Within your own environment, seek the limiting framework of those labels. For example, when you go to a restaurant, what labels and their associated assumptions do you carry about the waiters? Who are these people, more than simply labels that could be helpful in the future? What relational context can they offer? These are great practices for going to China. Reframing your labels into a broad relational context helps you think in the ways of the Chinese, who define themselves through relationships.

significantly more than the typical day at work. As you look to venture into the international business world, consider the box that may contain your thinking. Society containers or categories for your gender, role, ethnicity, or industry may not apply in China as they do in your country (one of the fundamental principles in China is the notion of equality within a communist state). Being a leader means not being contained by anyone's judgment. It also calls for a higher awareness of your judgments on others. Keep in mind that when you think outside the box, it only places you in another box. Why have boxes at all for any thought?

Transition from Industrial to Knowledge Economy

The major challenge facing developed countries may appear to be a global economic crisis. Under the surface of media attention, business systems from the industrial era struggle to function in a knowledge economy. The principles of management that govern many business practices and policies grew from the Industrial Revolution with concepts like Taylor's scientific principles of management. During the Industrial Revolution, labor was the primary resource. While the mechanistic principles were effective for labor resources, they do not meet the needs of a knowledge economy.[8,11]

Innovation is the name of the game in global business. It happens in processes, products, and services. The major commonality shared by the Chinese and Western societies is innovation. Both cultures have embraced innovation throughout their histories. From the invention of noodles and gunpowder in China to the creation of electricity and the automobile in America, knowledge is what propels economies. Business offers the medium for cultures to exchange knowledge. From this perspective, the traditional business principles meant to control people may not apply. Realizing the new medium of knowledge creation and management practices the principles of systems thinking.[10] Similar to the Chinese perspective on the interconnectedness of people, the knowledge economy seeks to balance the rigid containers of the past with the realization of non-linear human potential. Achieving a systemic awareness of the current business context empowers leaders with a choice to transform business systems. With the self-knowledge and experience of this transformation, Chinese leaders will perceive you with great respect and wisdom. Through these relational qualities, business ventures will be smooth and profitable.

I leave you with one thought to explore:

How can I transcend the limits of hierarchies to seek knowledge creation everywhere?

NOTES

1. Peter F. Drucker, *Managing in a Time of Great Change* (New York: Truman Talley Books, 1995).
2. John P. Kotter, *Leading Change* (Boston: Harvard Business School Press, 1996).
3. Tess Reinhard, *A Grounded Theory Investigation of Change Leadership During Turbulent Times* (2007), in the ProQuest Dissertations & Theses: Full Text Database (UMI No. 3272165).
4. Richard S. DeFrank and John M. Ivancevich, "Stress on the Job: An Executive Update," *Academy of Management Executive*, 12(3) (1998): 55–66.
5. Roland G. Robertson, *Rotting Face: Smallpox and the American Indian* (Caldwell, ID: Caxton Press, 2001)
6. Kalorama, "The World Market for Pain Management Drugs and Devices" (Lead Discovery, 2006), https://www.leaddiscovery.co.uk/Reports/105 (accessed February 22, 2009).
7. Carl Harshman and Ellen Harshman, "The Gordian Knot of Ethics: Understanding Leadership Effectiveness and Ethical Behavior," *Journal of Business Ethics*, 78(1/2), (March 2008): 175–92.
8. James G. Clawson, *Level Three Leadership: Getting Below the Surface*, 3rd ed. (New York: Pearson, 2006).
9. Sumantra Ghoshal, "Bad Management Theories Are Destroying Good Management Practices," *Academy of Management Learning & Education*, 4(1), (March 2005): 75–91.
10. Peter Checkland, *Systems Thinking, Systems Practice: A 30-Year Retrospective* (New York: John Wiley & Sons, Inc., 1999).
11. Roy Jacques, *Manufacturing the Employee: Management Knowledge from the 19th to 21st Centuries* (Thousand Oaks, CA: Sage Publications, 1996).

12. Needham High School's World History Web Site, "Child Labor in Factories: A New Workforce during the Industrial Revolution," Needham High School, http://nhs.needham.k12.ma.us/cur/Baker_00/2002_p7/ak_p7/childlabor.

13. John D. Blackburn, Elliot I. Klayman, and Martin H. Malin, *The Legal Environment of Business*, (Boston: Irwin, 1994).

EASTERN BELIEFS
AND VALUES

China's history is one of the oldest in the world. Starting in 2070 BCE, the Xia dynasty established the formal beginnings of China's rich history. This is a history of numerous unifications and separations. As a nation of many states, the Qin dynasty (221 BCE to 207 BCE) was the first to unify China and establish a national currency, written language, and standard weights and measures. While this was one of the shorter dynasties with only 15 years, it laid a solid foundation for many aspects of China's politics, culture, and economy. Throughout China's history, many forces separated and unified the nation. While China had its share of foreign battles such as those with the Japanese and Mongols, many of the separations were due to its own leaders, who sought control of the country.[1]

One of the most profound foundations in China often missed is the significant difference between Western beliefs of royal blood and China's belief that any man can rise from the peasants and become a king. As early as 206 BCE, Lui Bang was the founder of the western Han dynasty. This is the first precedent for someone of a common family to climb to the top and become an emperor. Even with limited educational or family background, Bang used his talents and a bold vision to rule. Being consistent with his journey, he also employed many others with great talent from the grass-roots level. His crucial leaders such as generals and ministers were all commoners at one time. Other major leaders of China, such as Emperor Taizu (or Zhu Yuanzhang) in the Ming dynasty (1368–1644) and Chairman Mao, were all born in peasant families. Can you even imagine that at one time, the young emperor Taizu was a beggar on the streets? Later, he became a courageous and resourceful leader who fought the Mongols and reunified China.[1] These and many other historical facts lay the fundamental groundwork for Chinese values and beliefs. While many Western civilizations developed with kings and queens (royal blood), the Chinese have a significant history (over 2,200 years) in living with the belief that any man could become the nation's leader. The depth of such a belief makes a dramatic influence on business practices.

Chinese Values Overview

When looking at the practices of Chinese business leaders, one might associate the surface characteristics of a focus on task or performance. From conventional wisdom, the visible behaviors include ensuring a clear focus on goals and objectives, emphasizing rules and procedures, accentuating high standards, and securing meaningful relationships. Underneath the visible behaviors lies a complex combination of Western influences, communist ideologies, and a rich traditional Chinese culture including Confucianism, Taoism, and Buddhism. One of the foundations of this book is the understanding that China is not a simple homogenous culture, with one set of values and beliefs applicable to all people. While many may appear to be Chinese "looking" on the surface to the Western eyes, each individual is unique depending on their heritage, gender, upbringing, educational level, spiritual and philosophical beliefs, and socioeconomic status. The rich historical context of China requires a high level of awareness and an ability to understand the unique values and beliefs of the individual. The information in this chapter provides initial guidelines for your exploration and understanding of this complexity. When you engage with Chinese business leaders, assuming the general applicability of this research on your relationship may not be completely accurate. Use the model described at the start of chapter 3 as a process guide to achieve deep understanding, which will yield successful relationships.

HEALTH

The top eight values selected by the 138 Chinese business leaders in the study accurately reflect the previous focus group outcomes. Health was by far the most important value to the Chinese people (see tables 3.3-1 and 3.3-2). Regardless of regional, gender, or generational differences, all groups chose health as the dominant value. Within the historical background of China, two basic drivers influence this preference. The first is the fundamental principle of caring for its people. China's history is one of the first to embody significant thought on the importance of its people. One popular saying states, "People are the root of a country, and, when the root is firm, the country is tranquil." Confucian philosophy has its foundation in putting people first.[1] With the rich underlying theme of people as the core of a country, the health of the people is naturally a primary concern. This definition of health is far beyond the conventional perspective of physical health or weight control. Emotional and psychological concepts such as inner harmony, pride, happiness, and honor are all part of the sphere of health.

Table 3.3-1. Top Eight Values by points (out of 138 participants).

	Value	Point Rating
1.	Health	10.46%
2.	Family	9.14%
3.	Career	6.32%
4.	Personal Achievement	5.13%
5.	Fun/Happiness	4.54%
6.	Competence	4.52%
7.	Competition	3.34%
8.	Responsibility	3.12%
	Total	46.57%

Table 3.3-2. Top Eight Values by frequency of selection (out of 1,104 selections).

	Value	Frequency Rating
1.	Health	8.06%
2.	Family	6.79%
3.	Career	5.07%
4.	Fun/Happiness	4.35%
5.	Competence	4.26%
6.	Personal Achievement	4.17%
7.	Competition	3.62%
8.	Inner Harmony	2.99%
	Total	39.31%

The second driver for health is the challenging times during the 1950s through the 1970s. During that period, the collective farming system had a perpetual shortage of food grain.[2] Having to feed a population that went from 570 million in 1952 to just under a billion (968 million) by 1979 created shortages in various regions of China, that in turn created significant health concerns. I vividly remember my family making sure that I ate every grain of rice in my bowl (equivalent of a plate in Western societies). With a scarcity mentality, food was always cherished. No one had to use phrases like "there are people starving in other parts of the world" to convince people not to waste food. Everything was eaten. This is also one of the reasons why the Chinese value many delicacies that are grotesque to the Western appetite. When there was not enough food, the innovative culture created many strategies to make anything appetizing.

From a Chinese socioeconomic perspective, people who are wealthy are often overweight. The basic assumption behind the wealth of "weight" is that a family has ample resources to feed themselves abundantly. Still today, many older generations tend to judge one's success by the amount of weight one carries. For example, every time I see my grandmother (who is almost 90 years old and grew up in the old China), one of the first comments out of her mouth is that I've lost weight. Being physically fit and healthy by Western standards does not yield positive reactions from the older generation who grew up at a time when food was scarce. While she realizes the lack of alignment between the perceived wealth of weight and actual wealth and success, the significant influences of the challenging decades continue to lead to reactionary behaviors. The younger generations may not have as strong a sense of this, but they are still taught by the older generations. Health will continue to have a special relationship to food and weight for many generations to come.

FAMILY

Family is the second most important value. Aside from the city of Anhui, which placed career slightly above health, family closely follows health in all other regions. No differences existed in gender or generations. While relationships are important in all aspects of Chinese society, the relationships within families are even more crucial. Since the family is the basic operating unit, people spend a great deal of time on the hierarchy within the family. It is common to hire family members in one's business, for example. In some companies, the wife and husband run two separate aspects of the company. Shanghai First International Logistics Company is a great example of a successful organization with the husband performing the duties of a CEO and the wife performing the duties of a COO. The family hierarchy translates well into the business setting to allow fluid and efficient business decisions.

In comparison to Westerners who selected family as the top value, the definition of the value among Chinese is unique. A closer look at the definitions of family reveals the drastic differences. Five specific perspectives on family composed the value of family in the second phase of the survey: Family Time, Closeness, Work-Family Connection, Achievement-Family Connection, and Family Proud of Work (see details in table 3.3-3).

According to the sample of Western business leaders, family time and closeness had the highest level of importance. The interesting aspect of the findings saw a low level of importance when connected to work. Most of the participants saw the relationship to work as slightly unimportant to slightly important. The Chinese business leaders, on the other hand, saw a stronger connection between work and family. Looking at the results in table 3.3-4, work's connection to family is higher. This finding further supports the notion of family within the workplace.

Further study into this phenomenon reveals a high level of congruence between the value of connectivity of family-work and corresponding behaviors (at 75.91%—one of the highest levels across all dimensions of values and beliefs within the study). The congruence between family and behaviors is nearly five points above that of Westerners (see table 3.3-5).

Table 3.3-3. Variable descriptions to assessing the definition of family.

Variable name	Description
Family Time	The importance of spending time with family.
Closeness	Having a close relationship with other family members.
Work-Family Connection	Viewing work and family as connected aspect of life. Work is for the success of the family.
Achievement-Family Connection	Family is one definition of achievement in life.
Family Proud of Work	Working hard yields family pride. Another perspective on the role that works plays within the family.

Aside from the top values, Chinese had a smaller set of values that did not get any attention. In common with Westerners, intensity is one of the two. Religion was the other value that did not receive any attention from any of the 138 business leaders (see table 3.3-6). At the same time, Westerners rated religion as the 24th most important value, tied with inner harmony. The Chinese rated inner harmony to be within the top ten.

While this may be surprising to many Westerners, Chinese culture is rich with philosophies of life without an association to an organized form of religion. Many of the principles in Christianity align with philosophies of Confucius, Buddha, and Lao Tzu. While these philosophies have had a significant impact on the Chinese culture for over 200 years, they do not call for a physical place of worship.[3] Instead, these philosophies act as a guide for everyday actions and decisions.

REGIONAL DIFFERENCES ON VALUES

The regional comparison of top values divulges the uniqueness of three different cities. Two reasons exist for the selection of cities. Strategic importance on the business level was the first consideration. Since Shanghai is one of the primary business centers in China, its inclusion illustrates business leaders' values within a city that never sleeps, especially when it comes to the continuous construction of skyscrapers. Beijing is the capital city, which is also of strategic importance when conducting business. Many national policies and regulations on foreign trade come from the capital city. Anhui also provides great insight as it is located close to Shanghai, just under 300 miles or over 450 kilometers in driving distance. It illustrates the uniqueness of values between two regions.

The second consideration is the accessibility of participants. As with any major study, the best designs are worthless without getting meaningful participants. Powerful relationships were crucial to getting participants. Shanghai offered many relationships due to a high concentration of my family members in the area. Beijing had a combination of business and family

Table 3.3-4. Ratings of different family variables.

	Family Time	Closeness	Work-Family Connection	Achievement-Family Connection	Family Proud of Work
Western Perspectives	5.48	5.55	**3.42**	4.58	3.73
Chinese Perspectives	4.79	5.46	**4.54**	4.35	4.29

Table 3.3-5. Congruence scores of different family variables.

	Family Time	Closeness	Work-Family Connection	Achievement-Family Connection	Family Proud of Work	Overall Congruence
Western Perspectives	57.83%	60.91%	67.88%	67.60%	**70.20%**	64.88%
Chinese Perspectives	67.46%	70.79%	**75.91%**	73.27%	61.42%	69.77%

Table 3.3-6. Unselected values out of 1,104 values chosen as important.

Chinese Perspectives	Western Perspectives
Intensity	Authority
Religion	Change
	Competition
	Decisiveness
	Fame
	Intensity
	Perfection
	Structure

relationships. Anhui had one key strategic relationship thanks to my mother and her former school friend's daughter, who is a successful entrepreneur.

As seen in table 3.3-7, the regional uniqueness is fascinating. Overall, Beijing had the highest total percentage of value frequency at 50.46%. This illustrates the homogeneity of its population with similar values. Shanghai on the other hand, being a major international business center, has a much wider spread of core values with a total of only 36%. While all regions agreed on health as the most important, they each had a unique set of values that did not appear on others' lists. Anhui claimed career as the second most important value, while the other two regions showed career as number four priority. With the strong connection between family and work from the definition of family, career and family are closely related. The third value difference between Beijing and Shanghai was profound. In Beijing, people appeared to value personal achievement while none of the other regions had this value in their top eight list. The latest developments in Beijing, especially with the 2008 Olympics, could be a significant influence on leading its people towards its potential as a world leader. In contrast, Shanghai claimed wisdom as its third most important value, which was not in the other two regions' top eight list. As one of the most populous and oldest cities, Shanghai is unique in many ways. Even amongst the Chinese people, various regions maintain their unique perspectives about people from Shanghai compared to other parts of China. The findings of unique values reflect this perspective, as Shanghai had four specific values that did not appear in the other two regions' top eight lists.

From a practical perspective, working with business leaders in Beijing requires different strategies than does working with business leaders in Shanghai. When working with people who highly value personal achievement, strategies should focus on the ambitions of those involved. On the other hand, working with leaders in Shanghai will require depth of knowledge and understanding. Since they highly value wisdom, grounded individuals with a high sense of self as well as a global consciousness of the business systems in concert would yield the respect of Shanghai business leaders.

This value is much more complex for Western leaders to grasp than is personal achievement. Wisdom from the Chinese philosophies calls for a

Table 3.3-7. Regional comparison of top values by frequency.

Anhui	(n = 296)	Beijing	(n = 504)	Shanghai	(n = 208)
Health	8.11%	Health	11.15%	Health	7.69%
Career	7.43%	Family	10.69%	Family	6.73%
Family	6.76%	**Personal Achievement**	5.86%	**Wisdom**	5.29%
Competence	5.41%	Career	5.52%	Career	3.85%
Fun/Happiness	4.39%	Fun/Happiness	5.17%	**Freedom**	3.37%
Inner Harmony	3.72%	Competence	4.14%	Fun/Happiness	3.37%
Integrity	3.72%	Inner Harmony	4.14%	**Comfort**	2.88%
Knowledge	3.72%	Responsibility	3.79%	**Friendship**	2.88%
Totals	43.24%		50.46%		36.06%

world sense of harmony, in addition to understanding one's journey and the respective role required within the system of relationships. I understand that wisdom is a tough concept to define or grasp within Western societies. Learning to practice wise business decisions from a Chinese perspective is even more challenging. In my journey to writing this book, the initial thought was to provide intellectual data that would help Western managers succeed in China. But I also began to realize that this book isn't just an intellectual pursuit, but also a development of wisdom so that one can gain the trust and respect of an ancient culture. There are many smart people in the world, but very few understand and live in wisdom.

GENDER DIFFERENCES ON VALUES

The Chinese culture has deep roots in a patriarchy. Within the basic operating unit of family, the males often enjoyed an unalienable authority over females of the same generation. Typically, the head of the household is a position controlled by the oldest male of the family. Even within the family of a married couple, the family of the husband is considered "inside" while the family of the wife is considered "outside." The names of uncles, aunts, and grandparents all reflect this principle. Within the business world, the differences between males and females are obvious. While I was facilitating a group activity with 35 managers and executives, the females did not make any statements in a challenging task that called for collaboration. While all members of the group held valuable information, I specifically did not choose a positional leader. Within minutes, the conversations between dominant males led the group without any female input. This

■ MIND GEM 3.3 ■

Mind Gem 3.3: How do you know if you have wisdom? The definition of wisdom from a dictionary is rather ambiguous. Wisdom has multiple dimensions within multiple intelligences.[4] In addition to the depth of intelligence within each dimension, the connectivity between the multiple intelligences in how they work together is another layer of wisdom (systemic perspective). Adopting the model from my previous book, let's look at five perspectives of wisdom.[5] The intellectual perspective focuses on the analytical and logical depth of intelligence; emotional perspective focuses on emotional depth; spiritual perspective is a depth of understanding in one's purpose and connection to a higher power; somatic perspective seeks an understanding of one's physical reactions to various states (i.e., what your body does when you get stressed). I cannot make comments on this document, but should the 5th perspective be detailed in this list?

Tactical steps:

These questions are not simple to answer. Take the time to reflect on each question with depth within yourself. While

continued on page 94

continued from page 93

external sources can provide definitions, your internal interpretation of each is the primary focus of this wise activity.

1. What is wisdom from an intellectual perspective?

   a. How would I develop my depth of knowledge? There is much more to wisdom than knowledge of something.

2. What is wisdom from an emotional perspective?

   a. What steps do I need to take to ground myself emotionally? How can I be a solid stronghold emotionally when turbulent changes are all around?

   b. How might my journey in emotional development reflect wisdom?

3. What is wisdom from a spiritual perspective?

   a. How lost should I be within the journey towards a greater purpose?

   b. How can I silence my mind to hear the wisdom of my soul?

4. What is wisdom from a somatic perspective?

   a. How aware am I of the physical changes in my

continued on page 95

experience reflects the traditional family roles played in a patriarchy.

The analysis of male and female values sets illustrates some differences of priority. For men, career and happiness were more important than competence. It was rather interesting to see that women rate competence as the number three priority. Influenced by the Western principles of equality, their pursuit of equality takes shape in their increased competence and knowledge.

Competition reared its head in the male value set. This is a very interesting phenomenon since the Chinese culture traditionally seeks harmony. The influences of the Western world along with capitalist principles push the Chinese culture to be more competitive in the global marketplace. At the same time, their tradition of harmony restrains the Chinese from open competition, resulting in indirect strategies to compete.[3] Within this group of 63 male business leaders, the priority list places competition over inner harmony. At the same time, if being in harmony with others defines family and happiness, competition is still lower in priority.

More interestingly, the group of Western business leaders did not select competition at all as any of their top eight values. Could this reflect the perceived economic position of Western societies? Since they are on top of the world economic powers, competition is not something they'd desire from anyone else. Or could it reflect a lack of desire to compete in a reality that is constantly focused on competition with one's neighbors?

From a practical perspective, working with male or female business leaders in China calls for different strategies. When working with males, career, happiness, and competition require conscious thought for another's development path in specific positions of influence. Females on the other hand would enjoy consideration of competence development from a knowledge perspective.

Table 3.3-8. Gender comparison of top values by frequency.

Male Values	Frequency	Female Values	Frequency
Health	7.02%	Health	8.50%
Family	6.01%	Family	7.33%
Career	5.06%	Competence	5.00%
Fun/Happiness	4.39%	Career	4.50%
Competition	4.05%	Fun/Happiness	4.50%
Competence	3.91%	Personal Achievement	4.00%
Personal Achievement	3.64%	**Knowledge**	3.67%
Inner Harmony	2.97%	Responsibility	3.33%
Wisdom			

GENERATIONAL DIFFERENCES ON VALUES

China has three major generations in the workforce. The youngest generation is the 1980ers (born after the 1980s) with ages, as of this writing, from 18 to 29. The middle generation is the 1970ers (born after 1970). The oldest age group is those age 40 and above (also called 1960er generation). Although the legal retirement age is 60 for men and 55 for women, many retire earlier (in their forties or fifties), especially those working in state-owned organizations, to make room for the younger generations. The values and beliefs between the generations are greatly influenced by the dramatic changes China has gone through since 1979, when the reforms began. For a full understanding of the uniqueness in each generation, the cognitive development stages of a human being shed valuable insight.

According to a popular psychologist (Piaget), a human being has four stages of cognitive development. The *Sensorimotor* stage is the first, as children experience everything through their senses. Cognitive development begins to realize simple cause-effect relationships. After about two years of growth,

continued from page 94

body during shifts in situations and emotions? For example, am I aware of the increase in breathing when stressed?

b. How do I develop a slowness and awareness to my breathing?

5. What is wisdom from a systemic perspective? This is a perspective that provides insight into the connectivity between multiple intelligences within oneself.

a. How would I connect the multiple intelligences to function as a wise leader?

b. What steps are necessary to ensure that I see the connections from the individual to the business, as well as what is best for the world?

continued on page 96

continued from page 95

Your exploration in the realm of wisdom is unique to you. There is not a right or wrong answer, nor is there some Web site that offers the answers. Wisdom lies in your journey to dig further each time as you revisit this exercise.

children get into the *Preoperational* stage. Along with an explosion of language acquisition, children begin to make conclusions based on intuition and gut feeling with minimal understanding of other perspectives. The third stage is the *Concrete operations* stage. Starting at around the age of six, children begin to develop deductive reasoning. This reasoning is limited to concrete objects they experience in their lives. The final stage is the *Formal operations* stage, where teenagers begin to understand abstract concepts in addition to the concrete. All of these stages are a natural part of human development.[6] Now imagine the major changes in Chinese society that accompany these developmental stages. The beliefs developed about the world in one stage are now debunked at a later stage.

The 1960er generation had a challenging experience. While they are partially responsible for engineering the reforms, their fully developed cognition based on the old China of the 1960s through the 1970s had drastically changed. While growing up in a rigidly controlled communist environment, they're seeing the massive changes of capitalism as adults. They are learning to adapt to almost every aspect of life. While they were growing up, public displays of affection were not allowed. People wore the same exact color and only a couple of designs of coats. The common blue coat made individualism impossible in a sea of people. One married for life and divorce was unseen. The one major advantage that the 1960er generation had was its ability to understand abstract concepts like capitalism and economic reform that fueled the changes. They had the ability to relate abstract concepts to concrete events.

The 1970er generation is not as fortunate. While having gone through the first three stages of cognitive development before the economic reforms, their concrete operations stage established a set of beliefs about reality. But that was the reality before the reforms. In their formal operational stage, this generation had to dramatically reconfigure their lifestyle from scarcity to abundance. As they began to develop reasoning around abstract concepts, an assortment of traditional Chinese and Western principles sat on their plate. They were forced to make sense of the outcome of their first three stages of development and the new environment in their final stage of development. This experience also helped make this generation a powerhouse of thought in synthesizing the old and the new worlds. They are also a critical driving factor for the growth that China has experienced. Many of today's very successful innovators and entrepreneurs are of this generation (like Gary Wang of tudou, the Chinese equivalent of YouTube).[7]

The youngest generation (1980er) has had an easier transition into today's world. Those born early in this generation may have experienced some scarcity as reforms were beginning to take shape. At most, their *Preoperational* stage had to make some adjustments. Since their logical abilities had not yet developed, their life in the late 1980s shaped their reasoning with ample Western concepts. Today, public displays of affection are common amongst the younger generations. Vivid colors of clothing litter the landscape like tropical flowers. What was once a blue sea of blue coats (in the 1970s) is now a colorful and vibrant scene of developing youth. Along with the choices in clothing made possible by capitalism, the divorce rates have also accompanied the concept of more choices.

While this most predominant unit of operation has begun to show its weakness, the concept of loyalty is also on the edge. People in the younger generation (18-29 years old) tend to have similar job patterns to Western generation Xers and Yers. They change jobs every 2 to 5 years, seeking better pay and opportunity. The youngest generation has a life of abundance in most major cities. While under the one child rule, most of these people do not have siblings. Yet, for the first time in many decades in Chinese history, the abundance of food and clothing provided a "rich" childhood, especially when compared to the previous generations. As a result, many people in China consider this group to be a bit spoiled.

The historical changes of China's economic reforms had significant influence on the core values and beliefs of the generations. Aside from the alignment of the first two values, the lists of priorities by generation differ greatly (see table 3.3-9). The youngest generation is concerned with trust and comfort. Comfort as a value may reflect an abundance of necessities during their early years. Trust as a value is rather interesting, since relationships are a key aspect of Chinese culture. With the rapid economic development over the last couple of decades, trust can be a major concern for a less experienced and established workforce. Combined with a trend to switch jobs in pursuit of higher pay, trust plays a vital role in these turbulent job changes. An important value of historical significance that did not show up in the 18-29 year olds' top eight values list is inner harmony. Both the older two generations listed inner harmony. This may mark a slight shift in value systems due to Western influences.

The two older generations also listed competence as a core value. It makes sense to see competence in the 30-39 year olds since they are in the prime of their career development. The older generation's successes would place it lower in priority. One may wonder why the youngest generation did not have competence in their top values. While career and personal achievement are in the top four, competence is the natural foundation that provides for them. Could they be missing something of interest in their pursuit of career and achievement?

From a practical perspective, these generational differences are vital to working with Chinese business leaders. Understanding one's journey of development provides significant insight into what is important to an individual and why. For example, you're out to dinner with an executive who orders something that appears to be a delicacy. As host, he or she places it on your plate along with some other dishes. What could be the relational impact if

Table 3.3-9. Generational comparison of top values by frequency.

18–29 years old	Frequency	30–39 years old	Frequency	40+ years old	Frequency
Health	6.71%	Health	8.00%	Health	10.80%
Family	5.03%	Family	7.20%	Family	8.52%
Career	5.03%	**Competence**	4.96%	Career	7.39%
Personal Achievement	4.36%	Career	4.48%	Fun/Happiness	6.25%
Trust	4.03%	Fun/Happiness	4.16%	Personal Achievement	5.11%
Fun/Happiness	3.69%	Competition	4.00%	**Competence**	5.11%
Comfort	3.36%	Personal Achievement	3.84%	**Inner Harmony**	5.11%
Competition	3.36%	**Inner Harmony**	3.68%	**Respect**	3.98%
Totals	35.57%		40.32%		52.27%

you rejected the delicacy? If the executive grew up in a time when wasting food was forbidden due to a scarcity of food, it could send a clear message. Then again, depending on his or her adaptation to today's Chinese culture and Western cultures, it may not be as much of an issue logically. The one choice you'll have to make is to determine whether the individual makes decisions purely on logic, or does the reactionary programming from the old days drive decisions at a subconscious level? Often, basic subconscious triggers have a greater influence than one may admit. Being aware of people's historical past within their generation offers you a conscious choice not to put yourself at risk with something simple.

CHINA'S VALUE CONGRUENCE

The concept of congruence has slowly grown in popularity for a few decades in the Western world.[8,9] In 1955, Carl Rogers, an influential American psychologist, introduced the notion that individuals have an image of the ideal self. The distance between the ideal self and the experience of the workplace creates a level of congruence.[9] In China, the fundamentals of congruence have existed within the concept of harmony for thousands of years. Inner harmony defines one's ability to be at peace with self. Within the philosophies of many ancients (Confucius, Lao Tzu, Buddha), the Chinese culture strives for harmony. From an intrapersonal perspective, people take time to reflect and make conscious efforts to improve themselves. From an external perspective, harmony defines the ultimate goal, where people of the world live in peace.[1] Comparatively, inner harmony is on the top ten values list of the Chinese dataset, while it sits at number 24 in the Western dataset.

With this backdrop, the Chinese reflect a higher level of congruence at 66.5% compared to the Western level at 59.5%. A further breakdown of values congruence is shown in table 3.3-10. When looking at the regional comparisons, it's fascinating to see Beijing with a much lower congruence level than the other two cities. With a very successful 2008 Olympic games, Beijing is an awakening giant who's beginning to realize an even larger potential in itself. The countless innovations such as cleaning up the air for athletes and building the incredible structures showed the entire country what China is capable of doing when it puts its mind to it. This realization sets a new ideal self that stretches its distance from the experience of reality. The other demographic comparisons are relatively low. While females had a higher level of congruence than males, the 1970er generation had the highest amongst all three generations. The generational differences could also be explained by the cognitive development stages that Chinese history influenced. Since the 1970er generation had the most challenging experiences in synthesizing two worlds, their congruence level is slightly higher.

Going beyond the surface of averages, the congruence levels at different value priorities are not as consistent. The collected data allowed us to conduct an analysis of congruence at each degree of priority. We wanted to

Table 3.3-10. Values congruence averages by regional, gender, and generation groups.

	Average Congruence on Top Three Values
Anhui	72.80%
Beijing	**47.37%**
Shanghai	77.13%
Females	64.32%
Males	58.16%
1980er	59.61%
1970er	61.37%
1960er	55.38%

Table 3.3-11. Values congruence matrix for the first three values by regional, gender, and generation groups.

	1st Value Congruence	2nd Value Congruence	3rd Value Congruence
China Overall	58.66%	55.06%	72.48%
Anhui	72.64%	62.50%	83.26%
Beijing	**32.91%**	**45.43%**	**63.75%**
Shanghai	85.20%	74.04%	72.15%
Females	**62.18%**	**43.61%**	**87.17%**
Males	53.61%	53.65%	67.23%
1980er	**74.50%**	50.14%	54.18%
1970er	55.80%	48.98%	79.33%
1960er	44.75%	**81.42%**	39.96%

know how congruent people were for their top three values and what differences may exist. The result reveals the complexity of human nature that calls for individual understanding and not group categorization. Take the Beijing group for example—the results illustrate an increasing level of congruence as the priority level decreased. What rationale could you create to explain why it was easier to achieve congruence as the importance level decreased?

This trend did not hold true for other regions, genders, or generations. The female results showed the lowest level of congruence at the second value, while the highest was for the third value. On the other hand, the highest level of congruence was highest in the second value for the 1960er generation. These fascinating results call for numerous studies within each demographic. But I hope that the varying results between regions, generations, and genders illustrate the importance of seeing China one business leader at a time. Making assumptions about China as a whole or by any single group would lead to many potential errors that you cannot afford in a competitive global economy.

CHINA'S BELIEFS AND THEIR CONGRUENCE

Beliefs along with values drive the thought processes in business. They help shape the perception of an external event. Across the nine different belief dimensions, self-efficacy and relationships (see table 3.1-8 for detailed explanations of these beliefs) had the highest scores (see table 3.3-12). While the importance of relationships is well established in China, the belief in self-efficacy opens the possibility of success. Just a few decades ago, the belief in setting goals and reaching them was confined by a centralized system. Today, the higher level of confidence allows people to dream big, set goals, and take steps to reach them.

The two measures that were a bit challenging from conventional thought are demonstrated in the higher rating for individualism over collectivism. While other studies have found a high loyalty to one's community (collectivism), individualism was thought to be relatively lower in importance.[10] This study, however, found the importance of individualism to be more important than collectivism. Two possible explanations for this outcome are based on the organizational level of the study sample. First, the overwhelming majority of participants in the study were executives and professionals. Their level of success and their respective influences from Western cultures in business shifted their orientation. Second, the participants reside in major metropolitan areas where Western influences are significantly greater than in the vast rural regions of China.

To further understand the high degree of importance on individualism, a correlational analysis with self-efficacy revealed a positive relationship (correlation coefficient ranged 0.231 to 0.306). As people developed a higher sense of self and one's capabilities, the worth of the individual also increases.

DEMOGRAPHIC COMPARISONS OF BELIEFS AND THEIR CONGRUENCE

The regional comparisons illustrate the uniqueness of beliefs. Beijing and Shanghai, the larger cities, had a higher rating for self-efficacy (see table 3.3-13). More interestingly, Shanghai—a significant metropolitan business center—showed the lowest rating for individualism while collectivism was higher. This result contrasts with the other areas, since their individualism rating is higher

Table **3.3-12**. Beliefs and their respective congruence levels of Chinese business leaders (n = 138).

	Individualism	Self-Efficacy	Life Purpose	Power Distance	Paternalism	Collectivism	Proactivity	Relationships	Trust of Foreigners
Belief Ratings	**4.65**	4.30	4.04	4.51	*4.08*	3.88	*4.44*	**4.53**	4.30
Congruence	36.31%	41.67%	37.65%	43.20%	43.92%	33.70%	33.73%	39.84%	33.99%

Table **3.3-13**. Beliefs rating comparisons by region.

Region	Self-Efficacy	Life Purpose	Power Distance	Paternalism	Collectivism	Proactivity	Individualism	Relationships	Trust of Foreigners
Anhui	4.37	4.25	4.03	4.35	**4.01**	3.85	**4.32**	4.45	4.47
Beijing	**4.79**	4.30	4.06	4.58	**4.03**	3.95	**4.51**	4.56	4.29
Shanghai	**4.85**	3.74	3.88	4.42	**4.69**	4.46	**4.28**	4.42	4.06

Table 3.3-14. Congruence to beliefs comparisons by region.

Region	Overall Congruence
Anhui	30.95%
Beijing	24.16%
Shanghai	19.54%

than their collectivism rating. The uniqueness of beliefs in regions is another reason China isn't one simple culture.

In looking at the congruence values to beliefs by region, an inverse relationship appears (see table 3.3-14). As the size of the city gets larger, the lower the congruence level to beliefs. The outcome reflects the ambitions of large-city residents in China who are starting to have larger dreams, removing the mental ceiling created by pre-1979 policies.

The gender comparisons of beliefs revealed minimal differences. Both males and females had high ratings for self-efficacy and relationships (see table 3.3-15). Females had a higher rating for self-efficacy than men; a direct result of Western influences in business that boast equality between genders in theory.

The overall congruence levels to beliefs of each gender uncovered significant differences. According to the study, female business leaders are half as congruent as male business leaders (see table 3.3-16). From a theoretical perspective, the influences of the West on gender equality may exist in theory, but are not as significant in reality. The generations of beliefs and practices around male authority continue to limit the realization of the theory. This provides a *huge business opportunity*. Since females share similar beliefs with their male counterparts concerning personal abilities and roles in society, a business that addresses the low congruence would be very popular with female business leaders. The low level of congruence is a clear indication of market demand. Similar to the new business of developing emotional intelligence in leaders, the creation of business ventures to serve this psychological need can take shape from organizational development companies that provide training to individual development. As a nation going through a tremendous amount of change, balancing Western business principles and Chinese traditions with strategic wisdom creates a tremendous need and business opportunity.

From a generational perspective, the younger generations show a higher degree of self-efficacy (see table 3.3-17). This evidence supports the cognitive development stages perspective. As the younger generations were able to progress their final stage of cognitive development in and after the major economic reforms, they show a higher level of self-efficacy. The 1980er generation is the first to rival the Western perspective of self-efficacy (both rated self efficacy at 4.84).

Table 3.3-15. Beliefs rating comparisons by gender.

Gender	Self-Efficacy	Life Purpose	Power Distance	Paternalism	Collectivism	Proactivity	Individualism	Relationships	Trust of Foreigners
Female	**4.82**	4.43	4.11	4.64	4.09	4.03	4.49	**4.50**	4.21
Male	**4.49**	4.18	3.98	4.40	4.07	3.75	4.40	**4.54**	4.39

Table 3.3-16. Congruence to beliefs comparisons by gender.

Gender	Overall Congruence
Female	*15.88%*
Male	*38.87%*

As further support of the development stages perspective, the oldest generation also demonstrated the lowest level of individualism. The two other generations who had part of their final development stages occur within the last two decades both exhibit high levels of individualism.

The overall congruence to beliefs exposed the challenges of the middle generation in the workplace. They were by far the lowest in congruence, compared to the youngest (see table 3.3-18). Like the gender findings, this evidence shows significant opportunity for business. Since the people in this generation compose most of the middle- to high-level management in organizations, this is a profitable market with ample resources.

The demographic comparisons of values, beliefs, and their respective congruence uncover the complexity that exists in China. While people may appear to look similar, the underlying values and beliefs that drive decisions and behaviors are far more complex. As mentioned, under centralized control before 1979, all coats were one shade of blue. Today, clothing exists in countless colors. Such a transition in visible color mirrors the transformation of values and beliefs. While one could make some generalized categories, focus on the uniqueness of the Chinese business leader. Each individual has their root in traditional culture accompanied by many transforming influences from their region, their gender, their education, their experiences, and the West.

COMPARATIVE ANALYSIS—CHINA'S AND WESTERN VALUES AND BELIEF SYSTEMS

The overview of Western and Chinese value systems illustrates significant differences (see table 3.3-19). Both lists contain a number of values that do not appear in the top eight values of the other. While conventional thought challenges people to recognize the differences, it would be wise to also focus on the commonalities of the cultures so that one may establish strong business relationships.

Recently, I discussed the differences found within a leadership class composed of American business professionals. When family appeared at the top of the values list, a tenured law professor at a major educational institution had a rather unique perspective. He felt that the value of family is simply a mere excuse for individualism. While many people may use family as rationale for their decisions, they are basing most of their decisions on their personal needs. The family rationale only makes them feel good and justified.

Table 3.3-17. Beliefs rating comparisons by generation.

Generation	Self-Efficacy	Life Purpose	Power Distance	Paternalism	Collectivism	Proactivity	Individualism	Relationships	Trust of Foreigners
1980er	**4.84**	4.04	4.11	4.45	**4.41**	3.69	**4.48**	4.69	4.37
1970er	**4.60**	4.36	4.04	4.56	**4.01**	3.92	**4.50**	4.48	4.24
1960er	**4.51**	4.53	3.90	4.40	**3.81**	3.98	**4.13**	4.40	4.40

Table 3.3-18. Congruence to beliefs comparisons by generation.

Generation	Overall Congruence
1980er	53.43%
1970er	18.17%
1960er	29.72%

Table 3.3-19. Top eight values comparison between Chinese and Western perspectives.

Priority	Western Value System	Chinese Value System
1.	Family	Health
2.	**Integrity**	Family
3.	**Honesty**	**Career**
4.	Health	**Personal Achievement**
5.	Fun/Happiness	Fun/Happiness
6.	**Passion**	**Competence**
7.	**Trust**	**Competition**
8.	**Respect**	**Responsibility**

Whether you believe or refute it, the fascinating perspective is a great example of values interpretation. On the surface, the results suggest that family is highly valued by both Chinese and Western business leaders. Beneath the simple word, the definition of family and its application can vary drastically. Family has significant stronger relationships to work with the Chinese people. It also contributes to one's success in life. The behaviors behind family lead children to take care of their parents under one roof. While family is the top value in Western societies, one common practice is to send one's parents to senior homes or assisted-living communities. This practice leads to a common Chinese view that Westerners are much more selfish, always seeking their individual success without taking care of the old and the wise. This provides a great opportunity for Western managers to impress the Chinese, since the bar is set relatively low for family practices. Small gestures towards family and relationships with low expectations can yield significant respect.

Also from the comparison, the values of integrity and honesty did not make the Chinese values set. However, it does not mean that they do not value these characteristics. Their concept of health and family is highly relational. In order to create strong relationships, honesty and integrity are not separate from family. As a relational culture, Chinese people see the connectivity of individuals as a crucial part of success to live. In one dialogue with the founder of a technology company, Mr. Wang stated,

You have to put honesty in the first place; that will help you to build up a trusting bridge between you and your customers, and it gains more credit standing on your business . . . I have been doing business for over ten years, I always keep that fundamental as my philosophy, I will never let my partners and my staffs [be] disappointed, so, the integrity will be the first thing I need to do."[11]

Another values perspective is the congruence level. Overall, Chinese tend to have a higher level of congruence than Westerners (see table 3.3-20).

Digging deeper, the value of family reflects some differences. The Chinese dataset illustrates a higher degree of importance than the Western dataset (see table 3.3-21). Similarly, the level of congruence is also higher with the Chinese dataset. While the word family may appear at the top of both value systems, both indicators reveal some unique definitions and beliefs about family and its function in society.

The comparison between Chinese and Western beliefs exposed three major differences in beliefs (see table 3.3-22). While both groups did not place spirituality in the top 20 values, their belief in a higher calling showed the largest discrepancy. The other two differences in beliefs confirmed conventional thought on collectivism and proactivity. China is higher in collectivism than Western cultures are. With a need to define self in terms of relationships, it also scored lower on proactivity, which indicates one's belief about working on a task without input from others.

The last comparison was the congruence of beliefs. While the study uncovered China to have slightly higher levels of congruence with respect to values, it had a much lower congruence with respect to beliefs (see table 3.3-23). As a developing society with a mixture of thousand-year-old traditions and Western influences, the beliefs in China are slowly shifting.

Table 3.3-20. Congruence to the top eight values between Chinese and Western perspectives.

Chinese	Western
66.5%	59.5%

Table 3.3-21. A perspective of family between Chinese and Western perspectives.

	Chinese	Western
Degree of importance	*4.68*	*4.55*
Congruence	*69.77%*	*64.88%*

Table 3.3-22. Beliefs rating comparisons between Chinese and Western perspectives.

	Self Efficacy	Life Purpose	Power Distance	Paternalism	Collectivism	Proactivity	Individualism	Relationships	Trust of Foreigners
Chinese	4.65	**4.30**	4.04	4.51	**4.08**	**3.88**	4.44	4.53	4.30
Western	4.84	**4.95**	3.65	4.13	**3.53**	**4.45**	4.21	4.52	4.62

Table 3.3-23. Congruence of beliefs between Chinese and Western perspectives.

Chinese	Western
38.22%	54.06%

The comparison between the two cultures can go on endlessly. Situational variables would make a complex matrix of comparisons. For example, if you're a New York businessman, how does the set of values and beliefs compare to male business leaders in Shanghai who are of the 1970er generation? The large number of comparisons would only resemble the many fish that your stomach cannot digest at one sitting. The above data is an appetizer to the complexity of values and beliefs. It is your journey to learn to fish and determine the means to balance values and beliefs with the individuals you'll be working with.

NOTES

1. Jin Bo, *Understanding China: Introduction to China's History, Society and Culture* (Beijing, China: China Intercontinental Press, 2008).
2. Mengkui Wang, *China's Economy*, trans. Bingwen Lui (Beijing, China: China International Press, 2004).
3. Ming-Jer Chen, *Inside Chinese Business: A Guide for Managers Worldwide* (Boston, MA: Harvard Business Press, 2001).
4. Howard Gardner, *Multiple Intelligences: The Theory in Practice* (New York: Basic Books 1993).
5. Ted Sun, *Survival Tactics: Top 11 Behaviors of Successful Entrepreneurs* (Westport, CT: Greenwood Publishing Group, 2007).
6. Jeanne Ellis Ormrod, *Educational Psychology: Developing Learners*, 5th ed. (Upper Saddle River, NJ: Pearson 2006).
7. Rebecca Fannin, *Silicon Dragon: How China Is Winning the Tech Race* (New York: McGraw-Hill, 2007).
8. Lloyd C. Williams, *The Congruence of People and Organizations: Healing Dysfunction from the Inside Out* (Westport, CT: Quorum Books, 1993).
9. Lloyd C. Williams, *Creating the Congruence Workplace: Challenges for People and Their Organizations* (Westport, CT: Quorum Books, 2002).
10. Zeynep Aycan, Rabindra N. Kanungo, Manuel Mendonca, Kaicheng Yu, Jurgen Deller, Gunter Stahl and Anwar Kurshid, "Impact of Culture on Human Resource Management Practices: A 10-Country Comparison," *Applied Psychology: An International Review*, 49(1) (January 2000): 192.
11. Gary Wang, personal communication, October 2008.

3.4

CHINESE BUSINESS PRINCIPLES AND THEIR CHALLENGES

Commerce with foreign cultures is not a completely new concept for the modern China. While China was a closed country for many decades before the reforms in 1979, the Silk Road from the 3rd century BCE through the 17th century had many foreign interactions. Unfortunately, the period of 1840 to 1945 saw an abundance of lost wars with foreign powers. During these conflicts, China was forced to open unfair trading agreements with many nations and pay millions of pieces of silver to foreign powers such as Britain, Russia, Japan, and the United States. Since the end of World War II, when China won the first victory against a foreign power (Japan) in over a century, it has been very leery of opening its commerce to the outside world.[1,2] At every turn of business, government involvement continues to exist with a traditional and historical perspective.

The opening up to foreign investment and trade of China took a phased approach. Due to the vast land mass, billions of people, and many levels of economic development in various regions, the government of China wisely started the opening-up process with four special economic zones in south and southeast China (Shenzhen, Zhuhai, Shantou, and Xiamen) in 1980. Another 14 coastal cities officially opened in 1984. As more cities opened in later years, Deng Xiaoping, the chief architect of China's reform, declared a path towards a socialist market economy with unique Chinese characteristics.[1]

On November 10, 2001, the World Trade Organization granted membership to China. This accession shifted China's regional approach to opening up towards a multi-directional effort for modernization, creating transparency and access to compete on the global marketplace. One of the primary strategies for

China in this effort for modernization was to gain direct foreign investment. This has been a very successful strategy, as China boasts over 600,000 foreign-investment enterprises at the end of 2006 and over $700 billion dollars in direct investments, especially with the new policy system of foreign direct investment (FDI) that was approved in 2004.[1] This new policy emphasized the efficiency in the role that government played in enabling FDI.[3]

The Role of Government in Business

While there are countless articles and news stories on numerical data exhibiting the economic vitality of China, the context of business is not a free-market economy. The transition towards a socialist market economy may appear to have significant liberalization; the decentralization of government control still involves significant oversight within regional governments.[2,3] These controls are heavily influenced by the past (specifically 1840–1945). For example, the British launched a war in 1840, and won the first of many unequal treaties that forced China to trade with foreign nations. The Nanjung Treaty not only ceded Hong Kong to the British, it also forced China to open five major ports for trading and pay the British one-third of China's annual revenue. Over the next century, the British teamed up with a number of other nations including the United States, France, Japan, Russia, Italy, Germany, and Austria at various times to force further concessions. Plundering, killing, and burning of personal property characterized each invasion. At the end of each war, the Chinese government always had to pay a significant amount of money to foreign powers that would increase with each invasion.[1,2] Imagine a history of this magnitude by foreign powers on your land. How would you maintain control of your country from these experiences?

Based on the historical challenges of the Chinese government, the strict communist system maintained a tight control around all aspects of the economy. The latest reforms began to peel back the layers of control but still maintain strategic insight on most businesses as well as control over major industries such as auto manufacturing and telecommunications. Regardless of the level of control, smart business executives ensure that their relationships with supervisory agencies and party representatives are solid. A typical business may have over a dozen external relationship networks that influence its functions including, but not limited to, the legal system (local and national), taxation agency, auditing organizations, trade unions, government representatives at various levels of local and national government, financial institutions, and party representatives.[2] Due to the complexity of relationships in China, any major flawed decision can be heard within a village of millions in a short amount of time.

If you're looking to establish a business enterprise in China, it would be wise to leverage the existing relationships of leaders in your field. Since relationships between people have a historical past with multiple generations, the depth of relationships is much more significant than in the Western definition of relationship. Attempting to compete with new relationships will be an endless uphill battle. Furthermore, attempting to understand the many systems in operation from a theoretical perspective is nearly impossible, not to mention the addition of regional norms that may differ from explicit laws. For example, the Chinese socialist legal system has seven departments: 1) constitution and laws related to the constitution, 2) civil and commercial laws, 3) administrative laws, 4) economic laws, 5) social laws, 6) criminal laws, and finally, 7) procedure laws. Within each department of law, there are three levels of laws and regulations. In addition, Chinese characteristics are part of the system. Along with the legal system, the leadership of the Communist Party of China has nine different political parties that cooperate with each other and provide consultation to the government.[1] Knowing which department may direct you to a specific legal guideline, and figuring out how regional and local authorities govern the three levels of laws and regulations with Chinese characteristics, is a multifaceted beast. And we've not even gone into the nine-political-party system under the Communist Party leadership.

Rather than spending your valuable resources to understand a complex system and attempting to develop relationships yourself, seek local partners who know the lay of the land in both cultural and government systems.

Business Management and Challenges

In order to successfully manage a business, theories of management require a certain set of assumptions about the people it attempts to manage. In the transitional stage of China's economy, no single set of assumptions would hold true in most businesses. Most businesses will have workers from different parts of China. Many people from rural regions will have different expectations than people from urban centers. Workers from various generations will have unique values and beliefs amongst their generation. The abundance of new ventures from private businesses and foreign-interest enterprises has created a massive need for talented labor. Unfortunately, the educational system in the last 30 years has not been able to keep up with the many changes in China's economic environment. As a result, businesses experience increased turnover along with a war for talent.[4,5]

China's workforce is extremely diverse. From a regional perspective, many rural workers have flooded the urban workforce in search of a better life. Many of them take up blue-collar work such as being a taxi driver, a massage specialist, or a restaurant staff member. These people have a very different perspective on work. Their belief about work is drastically different than what most Westerners experience through many decades of prosperity. (Before moving forward, we'll have to direct your attention to the Western perspective of work. Many Westerners work to live; one could also argue that they live to work as well. This duality statement is too simple to quantify any culture.) Many Westerners' income often goes towards luxury items that are barely in the consciousness of these Chinese rural workers. With the significant discrepancies in economic development between urban centers and rural regions, many of these rural workers focus on feeding their families. As a result, they live to work. They work 10 to 12 hours each day, six to seven days each week. They live with a group of fellow workers in small rooms in order to save money for their families (8-12 people in a 10' x 10' room that is living room, bedroom, and dining room). Their work is often purely functional; most of these people are not concerned with smiling at customers. They simply perform the functional job and nothing more. Work is a pure, transactional exchange with nothing to smile about.

While at a restaurant eating with family members, I noticed the lack of a smile on the majority of the workers (mostly the assistant waiters and cleaning crew—they often have a head waiter who knows the language and menu well; the rest of the people are present for "service"). I decided to experiment with their morale (smiling). I directed a range of expressions at the various people. With some, I gave them a warm hello or a nod. At other times, I smiled at them with varying degrees. In multiple restaurants all over Shanghai, I was not successful at getting these workers to smile back. While there was always ample service from a functional perspective, the concept of smiling reflected their attitudes towards work. Perhaps I was a bit too naive to think that I could change their facial expressions with a single interaction. In comparison, these workers are like immigrants who enter the United States and work at the low paying jobs that U. S. citizens refuse to perform, except these workers in Shanghai are from the same country.

Urban workers are drastically different from rural workers. Customer service with a smile is part of the importance of relationships. Especially when they recognize the relationship you may have with prominent individuals, smiles and warm gestures are common. In general, these workers work to live. With reforms, Chinese people are able to obtain many of the products enjoyed by the West and more. Colorful clothing, advanced technology, choice of automobiles, and a variety of delicacies are just a few of the products Chinese people have come to enjoy.

Urban workers are a bit more complex from a management perspective than the rural workers. While rural workers have a single purpose for work, much like the workers of the Industrial Revolution, urban workers have varying expectations and desires for their employment. The simple exchange of money for service is far from sufficient, especially for the 1980er (18 to 29 years of age) and 1970er (30 to 39 years of age) generations. Having experienced the tremendous explosion of modernization at different ages of their cognitive development, these generations want more from life. These workers desire effective leadership, opportunity for accomplishment, advancement and recognition, a creative and fun workplace, team work, pride and interest in one's work, and, of course, compensation.[4]

The differences between the 1980er generation and 1970er generation also present a challenge. The younger generation tends to focus on the tangibles a lot more. Many have developed spending habits similar to the West (i.e., the majority of one's paycheck goes toward consumption). They tend to move from job to job much more often (every 2 to 4 years) than other generations, primarily seeking to maximize their income. The 1970er generation has a blend of traditional values and beliefs and those of the modern China. While they tend to stay with organizations longer than those from the 1980er generation, they also have a greater focus on career and family. Overall, the tendency for workers to stay with an organization has begun to diminish. A study found that up to 31 percent of mid-level and senior executives are very likely to leave their company. While professionals are at 18 percent, 24 percent of first-level supervisors and managers are very likely to leave.[4] This presents a massive challenge for organizations to maintain their human capital.

Before the days of reform, most organizations were state-owned enterprises that provided housing, education, and transportation for its workforce. While these organizations had significant challenges in efficiency and profitability, management was a heavy bureaucracy. Over the last three decades, hundreds of new private enterprises and foreign firms have drastically changed the landscape of work. How would one manage the diverse workforce of multiple generations with varying expectations? Management thinking and practices in China have not been able to keep up with the transformation, and some speculate that it might become the Achilles heel that slows down China's growth.[5] Others have estimated an approximate need of 75,000 effective managers over the next 15 years. The current figures tally only 5,000 managers.[6] Isn't it ironic for a nation of 1.3 billion people to be short on talented managers?

One of the strategies used by some organizations is to increase the "signing bonus." While cars can be an attractive offer for many, it creates a mentality that is loyal to money. In a country that greatly values relationships, such practices can upset the fabric of the culture. From the business perspective, using finances to attract talent takes away from the bottom line while training your workforce to be loyal to money. Instead, organizations could take the time to carefully study the intrinsic desires of the workforce and develop strategies consistent with those desires. From a contextual perspective, seeking to understand the workforce represents respect and care. The relational culture of China would embrace the efforts to build relationships and to enable development of the individual. Although limited, studies on job satisfaction have revealed intrinsic motivators, such as promotion, job interest, and fulfillment, as influential factors.[7] In the context of my study, these intrinsic work factors are closely connected to family. While it may be a bit more complex in organizational design, investment is minimal compared to the constant giving away of profits in the form of cars and other lavish gifts to retain and attract talent. Western principles of employee retention do not apply to the Chinese workforce, especially considering the unique values and beliefs in its culture.[5]

Contracts and Relationships

"Doing business in China is all about challenges, especially for Americans." This was the initial response of an entrepreneur attempting to do business in China. I'm not sure if you can read the frustration in his voice, but Matt was having a tough time; he had lost significant revenue from the lack of follow-through in product quality and consistency. After speaking with him, we realized some potential challenges in the Western thought process that did not apply to Chinese business.

In the Western world, a contract clearly outlines the details of a product or service. Payment terms often ensure that suppliers deliver the expected products. The Western business world also tends to look at businesses and people from a quantitative perspective. Hiring is done through skills assessment from resumes and past work history. I've always found it rather ironic that many people base decisions on resumes or marketing material, while the information on the documents may not accurately reflect the full truth. For example, up to 80 percent of resumes have some form of false information, according to a professor at The Ohio State University. Why are we so intent on using resumes and marketing materials as determinants for decisions? Where are the unbiased perspectives?

In China, contracts are part of relationships. A poor relationship will likely yield poor results, regardless of a contract. From a legal perspective, the Chinese legal system is relatively new compared to that of the West. Historically, the Chinese focused on inspiring behaviors through morality and harmony, not a legal doctrine. Since the opening up of China, integration with Western societies has created the basic framework of the lawyer system in 1996.[1] The concept of a contract guiding business transactions bounded by law still faces many challenges in this new system. Many foreign companies face a number of issues when conducting business in China. They include the challenges of keeping up with new regulations at national, provincial, and local levels; reluctance of Chinese business leaders to accept binding contracts; along with the lack of sanctity once a contract is present.[8] These challenges reflect an attempt to "squeeze a square peg in a round hole." The square peg is the Western rules of business by contracts; the round hole is the Chinese principles around relationships. They simply do not fit. The assumption made by many Western organizations going into China is what creates these challenges.

A full understanding of the relational business context in China rewards businesses with extreme efficiency. The secret to business success is rather simple! Relationships drive action. The depth of relationship provides significant respect and speed of action. Since the family is the basic unit, relationships within the family are crucial. Relationships between families can stretch back many generations. With this in mind, it is nearly impossible to compete with relationships that are generations old. So rather than attempting to compete, partnering with people with significant relational ties to key figures in business and government can gain you access to the network. These people are often the oldest males in a generation with a large immediate family (30 or more). Leveraging their knowledge and reputation is similar to having a key to the bank. They help navigate the constant reinterpretations and negotiations of a contract with greater ease.

Ethical Practices and Intellectual Property

One of the most common topics when speaking of China is the concern over losing intellectual property. In China, counterfeit brands are all over the place. It has come to a point where one of the favorite destinations of Western visitors is the counterfeit products market, where one can bargain for anything from "name brand" purses and clothing to electronics and movies. It's ironic to see that the majority of the shoppers in these markets are Westerners. Many Chinese people understand the poor quality of the products and do not make purchases. For example, as a skier, I had a need for a new ski jacket. In the United States, a name brand ski jacket would start at $200. While exploring those markets, I found many stores carrying name brands at minimal prices. My family members immediately informed me of the danger concerning the fabric used. "In a jacket, the lining needs to allow your body to breath. These fake jackets do not let your body breath, while they may feel and look like the real thing." With greater knowledge, shopping at these markets was no longer as interesting. This was also when I began to recognize the busloads of Western tourists shopping at these stores on a daily basis. So who is really supporting these counterfeit operations from the market side?

Beyond the surface of the ethical issue, many underlying forces influence intellectual property rights. From the cultural perspective, the traditional communist society sees knowledge as a community asset intended for the common good. Why should an organization horde knowledge for its own profits, especially when there's a need for better overall life for many in the country? This thinking also leads to a more practical perspective of socioeconomic stability. With over 800 million of out of the 1.3 billion living in rural areas, the ability to feed and clothe its people was a constant challenge for many decades. Continuing to overproduce products in addition to contractual agreements provides further income for a community. While minimal changes are made to the additional productions, it still provides necessities for the rural population. From this perspective, the decision may be between following an artificial rule created by foreigners that may enable social instability, or ignoring the rule to create an initial movement necessary to advance the population.

The socioeconomic perspective only provides a current view. Looking at it from a historical perspective, the Chinese are very connected to their past. During the years of 1840 through 1945, foreign powers forced China to pay over 740 million taels of silver and 66 million gold francs for war indemnity—wars that foreign powers initiated. During that time, numerous unfair policies ensured massive profitability of foreign organizations (e.g., one policy from the Xinchou Treaty in 1901 restricted any Chinese from establishing competition operations).[1] With over a century of brutality from foreign powers for economic dominance, has the West earned the right to impose more restrictions on the Chinese in their own country?

While the past may be a sensitive subject for many Chinese, government leaders also realize the need to maintain productive relationships with Western economies for the purposes of international commerce and mutual gain.

The underlying theme of great harmony is a foundation of Chinese pursuit. Within this foundation, harmony at the world level is attained through moral reasoning. Early revolutionary leaders such as Sun Yat-sen (1866–1925) challenged the Chinese people to strive for the equality of all people without class distinctions on a global level.[1] With this underlying philosophy, government leaders have worked diligently to crack down on intellectual property piracy. Many laws exist to protect intellectual property and branding; unfortunately, with such a large country and many provincial and local governments that profit from such activities, enforcement is a sizeable challenge. The movement is advancing. In 2000, while I was visiting, I could easily find counterfeit products on the streets of Shanghai. In 2008, I could not find them as easily. Many rural people in the streets will show you pictures to pique your interest, then lead you back into hidden display rooms. In many major cities, the crackdown has produced results.

Transition from Central Control to Knowledge Economy

The business context of China has changed drastically since the start of reform some 30 years ago. While the national government has delegated much of its control in business to provincial and local governments, it is still a major force of influence in all aspects of business. This has created a huge range of opportunities for both Chinese and foreign investors and entrepreneurs.

The past few decades saw hundreds of factories pop up in many rural regions. The next few decades will begin to see a shift toward a knowledge economy. As labor wages have already begun to increase in many parts of China, building factories in China has started to slow down. The Chinese have gone from being low-cost producers with many factories to being copycats who imitate existing technologies. And all of this is starting to shift. As a nation of innovations, gun powder and noodles from China transformed the Western world in ancient times. The present new technologies such as video streaming via mobile devices and the many innovations highlighted at the 2008 Olympics will continue to grow. The innovative culture will take the stage, presenting world-class inventors of new technologies.[9] These innovations don't come just from new technologies, but also in the form of applications. For example, the use of automobiles at the individual level is only a few decades old in China. Compared to the United States, the industry is in its infancy. Yet, I discovered something drastically different in almost every car that I thoroughly enjoyed. Each car seat had a head cushion that provided great comfort to my neck. While these commodities do not come with the cars, the majority of cars in Shanghai have these neck cushions. So I brought a couple back with me to the United States. Every friend who's sat in my car loved it. A thought occurred to me: why didn't we think of it? Why is it not in every single car?

The level of innovative thought will be one of the major economic drivers for China. Many global organizations like Oracle and Google have already established offices in China to capture both the creative minds of its people and the tremendous market share. Some of China's e-commerce sites have already overtaken major Western players like eBay, which was beaten by Alibaba.com in sales, and Amazon, which got outsmarted as a merchandising master by dangdang.com.[9] With close to 22 percent of the world's population and a shifting belief towards innovation in a transitioning socialist economy, the innovations from such a large pool of talent offer tremendous opportunity for any business venture. The biggest challenge rests in your ability to understand the culture and create effective relationships with respect and trust.

Do you have what it takes to partner with this accelerating economic powerhouse?

In the next section of the book, we will apply the research of values and beliefs on some basic fundamental compartments of business such as startup processes, marketing, and hiring practices. With each subsection, we will explore the rationale for business practices from both Western perspectives and Chinese perspectives. Depending on the region, gender, and generation, you may find a continuum of varying practices between the two perspectives. When you are done reading each subsection, the goal is not to simply give you the fish and assume that this fish will feed you throughout your business adventures in China. While you learn how to fish, I hope to leave you with more questions for personal exploration of individual uniqueness in China. In the context of the exploratory journey, you will develop an approach to understanding yourself, people in China, and much more.

NOTES

1. Jin Bo, *Understanding China: Introduction to China's History, Society and Culture* (Beijing, China: China Intercontinental Press, 2008).
2. Ming-Jer Chen, *Inside Chinese Business: A Guide for Managers Worldwide* (Boston: Harvard Business Press, 2001).
3. Li-ru Cheng and Xuan Zhou, "Characteristic of the New Policy System of Chinese Foreign Direct Investment," *China-USA Business Review*, 6(3) (March 2007): 19–22. (2007, March).
4. Development Dimensions International, Inc., "Employee Retention in China 2007: The Flight of Human Talent," *China Business Review* (July–August 2008).
5. Shaozhuang Ma and Virginia Trigo, "Winning the War for Managerial Talent in China: An Empirical Study," *Chinese Economy*, 41(3) (May 2008): 34–57.

6. Diana Farrell and Andrew J. Grant, "China's Looming Talent Shortage: The Emerging Global Labor Market," *McKinley Quarterly* (*The Online Journal of McKinley & Co.*), no. 4. (2005). http://www.dryvonnesum.com/pdf/China_Looming_Talent_Shortage_McKinsey_Qtrly_Oct_2005 (accessed March 15, 2009).

7. Florence Yean Yng Ling and Sook Ping, "Low Legal Risks Faced by Foreign Architectural, Engineering, and Construction Firms in China," *Journal of Professional Issues in Engineering Education & Practice*, 133(3) (July 2007): 238–45.

8. Rebecca Fannin, *Silicon Dragon: How China Is Winning the Tech Race* (New York: McGraw-Hill, 2007).

CHAPTER 4

BALANCING YOUR MIND IN TWO DIVERSE SYSTEMS

Are you a successful professional? Will you have success in international business ventures? Consider the context of these questions. What's the mental trap that limits your thinking?

As the section title suggests, the word *balance* requires existence in both worlds. The typical trap that many people fall into, as we've discussed many times before, is duality. Both questions above push you to see a duality and force a very simple yes/no response. As we've offered insights on the values and beliefs of both China and the Western perspective, it's clear the challenge is not merely take on one or the other. A simple right or wrong way of working with Chinese business leaders does not exist. Each individual may be unique to a given situation along with the relationship requirements. The objective is to create behaviors that balance your own values/beliefs and those of the Chinese. Thinking in a duality only forces you to make limited choices that can easily offend and terminate a business venture. Is it really necessary to impose a duality of thought in any given situation?

Conventional thought places China and the Western world on opposite extremes (East and West). In reality, many dimensions of thought between the two may overlap at times and oppose at other times. China has unique characteristics founded over 7,000 years of rich history, as figure 4.1 on the depth of the historical context indicates. With a conscious effort always to be connected with its past, many Chinese business practices are symbolic in nature. The Western perspective of business has gone through significant transformations from the Industrial Revolution to today's knowledge economy (as indicated by

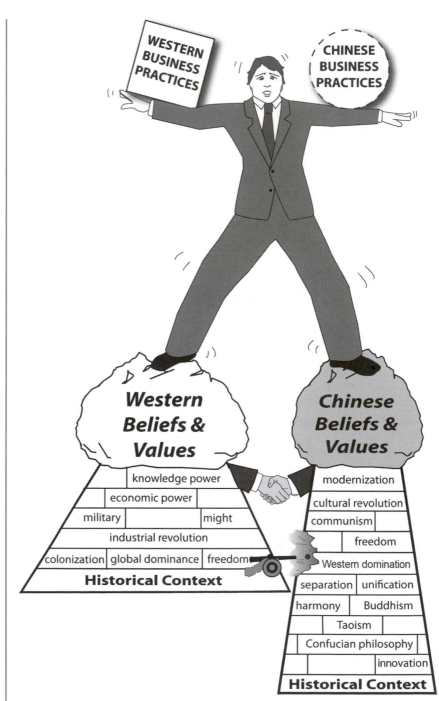

Figure 4.1. The multiple business contexts of both East and West challenge your thought processes.

the width of its historical foundation in figure 4.1). Objectivity, open markets, and profits are at the center of many Western business practices. The typical duality mentality challenges people to be in one world or another.

From the Chinese perspective, balance is part of a harmonious system. Balance is not a static concept where one achieves some level of equilibrium. Instead, the Chinese see balance as a constant readjustment and adaptation to changes. Going back to ancient philosophy (Lao Tzu), the element of water represents flexibility and adaptability due to the constant changes of the environment.[1] The concept of balance in this chapter of the book has the same context as Lao Tzu. Balance is a constant adaptation through understanding of the individuals involved along with situational influences.

Duality creates absolutes that limit human potential. In the case of international business, it can easily lead toward major conflicts. If someone asked you "Are you a leader or a manager?" how would you respond? Could you challenge the idea of duality embedded in the question?

Duality from Reductionism

When engaging Chinese business leaders, learning to live within both worlds is the key to success. One major impediment is the common practice of reductionism. Although this is an academic term, it signifies the separation of parts and their analysis to understand the whole. In the industrial era, the concept led to major innovations since the major source of output was by machines and linear assembly lines. Today's major competitive resource is knowledge. With organic units of production, reductionism eliminates the intricacies of relationships. In our knowledge-based economy, reductionism creates problems. Separation of negative emotions in the workplace, for example, leads to high stress. Separation of family from one's "professional" behaviors enables significant loss of identity that may lead to high interpersonal conflict and a lack of work-life balance. As you enter the world of Chinese society, reductionist thinking can be limiting as well in a relational culture full of attention to connections and not just the parts of the whole.

So should you believe in this old saying "When in Rome, do as the Romans do"? From a historical perspective, St. Ambrose, Bishop of Milan, made this statement in reference to fasting on Saturday when in Rome, but not in Milan.[2] Since this simple application in 387 CE, the concept has been widely used in many aspects of society. The major challenge with such a philosophy is the loss of one's identity. Can you really be someone else by altering simple behaviors? Be careful how you might answer this one. For example, if you were to behave like a Chinese businessperson, you might find yourself eating some delicacies and practicing some unusual rituals that would be found only on reality TV shows in the United States. Would this really mean that the Chinese might accept you as one of their own? Furthermore, the Chinese find it intellectually stimulating and interesting to learn about another culture. If you behave as they do, the fun of business could be lost. Practicing the old saying about being in Rome may not yield the desired outcomes.

The concept of being in both worlds is challenging. It is nearly impossible to remove the mental framework of reductionism by reading a book. I've had many workshops with leaders on shifting their mind into multiplicity so that they can stop reacting to situations and respond wisely instead. Especially in emotionally challenging contexts, most people resort to what they've been taught and grown up with for many decades. Here are two exercises that challenge some existing paradigms to prepare you for transitioning from duality to multiplicity in thought.

The table below highlights some common concepts or issues people face. In the second column, see if you can identify the duality that limits your thought or existence. Some of these concepts also contain simplistic and linear cause and effect. In the final column, challenge yourself to create a new concept derived from multiplicity. For example, a financial expert might ask, "Are you saving enough for your retirement?" From a conventional perspective, most people are concerned with diminishing funds in many social security systems. As a result, they save each month for retirement. The duality in the concept is whether or not to save for retirement. The mental trap is the concept of retirement—does it really exist? Choosing to see retirement through unconventional wisdom could redefine the concept within the knowledge economy. When it came to the industrial era, retirement was necessary since labor (muscle) was the primary resource. Today, the primary resource is knowledge/innovation. This resource comes from one's brain. If one's brain retires, then there is no more life. What if "retirement" is a reduction of hours spent on work while increasing one's income per hour? You could strive to work less each year per week while making more per hour each year. What options are available for this concept of retirement? You can make a conscious choice to depart duality existence.

Balancing the business practices of both worlds requires multiplicity. Many traditional studies have pitted Western business practices on the opposite side

Table 4.1. Developing your thought process in multiplicity.

1. Conventional Thought	2. What is the duality in each?	3. Unconventional Wisdom (Multiplicity)
Glass Half Full or Empty		
Thinking Outside the Box		
Head / Back Ache – Take a Pill		
Work-Life Balance		
Workplace Stress		

of Chinese business practices. While statistical averages exist, the individual you're working with is unlikely to behave according to such numerical representations in all dimensions.[3] The probability of this may have been higher in the early years of China's modernization (early 1980s); today's China is a complex mix of practices depending on many factors such as generation, experience with Westerners, socioeconomic upbringing, and regional residence (many aspects of multiplicity). In order to balance many sides, not just two, the first duty of a responsible business leader resides within the context of understanding the individual of interest. I've developed a simple tool (figure 4.2) for you to explore as you meet Chinese business leaders. Notice that it has two extremes for each belief. People do not exist within one extreme at all times. Different situations can lead people to behave within the continuum between the two end points. The most interesting aspect about multiplicity is the combination of various beliefs working in concert at a given situation. Layering beliefs on top of each other illustrates the complexity of the matrix of beliefs.

The tool contains some basic beliefs that drive behavior. If you have a team, consider making copies of this scale and gather the unique perspective of the team on how each individual perceives Chinese business leaders. This would provide you with a scientific perspective on an individual's belief system. These beliefs drive all dimensions of business; an in-depth comprehension enables strategic insight on business relationships.

Cultural Beliefs Discovery Plan

Figure 4.2 is a quick graphical tool to assess individuals of interest. This tool isn't just for working with business leaders from other cultures. It can also be used to understand people in your everyday life. One method of analysis includes two simple steps. Ask another individual to complete the scale on his or her own, while you complete it based on your experiences with the individual. Then compare the two and explore further in conversations.

Another method uses shapes as markers on the scale to compare various other beliefs with your own (see figure 4.3). You can rate these dimensions for your beliefs with a small square. As you meet and work with others, rate their beliefs with circles, triangles, etc. to denote different individuals based on position, gender, and ethnic backgrounds. The applications of this tool are numerous. The intent is to provide a guide to understanding others. From a strategic perspective for understanding, you can create a list of starter questions for each of the eight dimensions. Over a meal, have a conversation about each dimension with the starter question. This is where you'll begin to learn to catch some big fish. The bait is the questions you'll design. The fish you're looking to catch is the knowledge of beliefs inside the ocean of thoughts within the individual. Below is the contextual framework for the specific tactics for understanding.

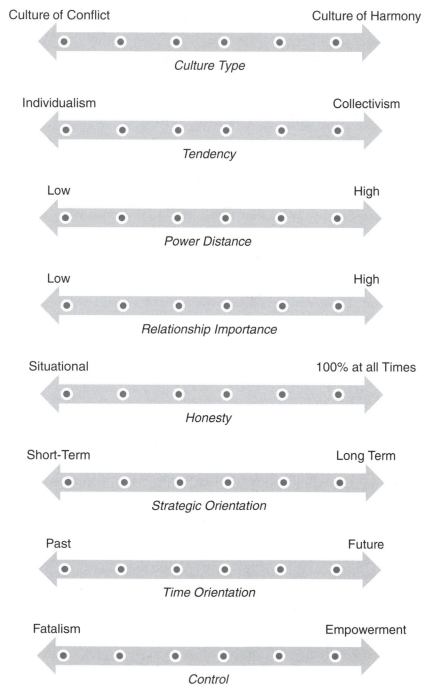

Cultural Beliefs Discovery

Culture of Conflict — Culture of Harmony
Culture Type

Individualism — Collectivism
Tendency

Low — High
Power Distance

Low — High
Relationship Importance

Situational — 100% at all Times
Honesty

Short-Term — Long Term
Strategic Orientation

Past — Future
Time Orientation

Fatalism — Empowerment
Control

Figure 4.2. A simple tool for discovering individual beliefs.

Example Application:

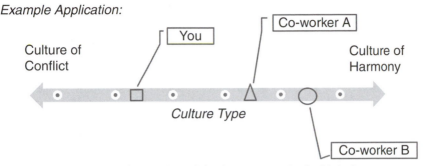

Figure 4.3. An example of using the tool for discovering individual beliefs.

CULTURAL BELIEFS DISCOVERY PLAN

1. Plan specific questions that lead towards discovery for each dimension. Ensure that each question is an open-ended question.
   a. Culture Type: When you have a disagreement with people, how do you tend to handle the situation?
   b. Tendency: What choice do you make when the organization's needs are in conflict with your personal needs?
   c. Power Distance: (I'll leave the rest of the dimensions to your creative mind. If I gave you the questions for each, they would be my words and not your own. Creating your own questions empowers you to develop those skills for any given situation.)
   d. Relationships . . . and so on for the other dimensions.
2. Since the Chinese culture has a strong orientation to meals, strategically engage in a conversation about one or two specific dimensions in which to seek understanding over lunch or dinner. Ask the planned question when appropriate. Please keep in mind that the context of these deep questions builds powerful relationships. Thought-provoking questions reflect respect and interest for an individual's culture and beliefs.
   a. Create follow-up questions based on the response. Dig deeper with any cultural issues that may appear. You may want to start with soft requests such as "Help me understand your rationale for . . ."
   b. Consider taking this on at least two perspectives. The historical perspective illustrates the individual's connection to China's past. The cultural perspective illustrates the individual's view of their own personal experiences in life. Some questions (bait) to catch meaningful and "big" fish are as follows:
      i. How has China's history influenced this belief?
      ii. What have you experienced personally to arrive at this belief?
3. Immediately after the meal, pull out the tool and mark down what you've learned along with some notes on the side for specific content.

4. Repeat this plan for other dimensions of interest.
5. Once you have a better understanding of these beliefs and their corresponding rationale from both a cultural and historical perspective, design your communications to maintain content consistency with your needs, but contextual requirements of the Chinese business leader of interest. This will help you exist on both sides of the diverse worlds.

Many studies place their findings as statistical results that paint a general picture of these dimensions. While these reports give you a sizable "fish" in data, they lack the flavor that make them meaningful. The *Cultural Beliefs Discovery Plan* is a method to catch your own fish while also providing you with a strategic approach to building meaningful and respectful relationships. As you explore the Chinese culture, you'll find that these dimensions are much more complex than placing one culture at one extreme and the other at the opposite end (not at all a simple duality). Even within the same cultures, people exist within the continuum of the ratings based on individuals and situations (multiplicity). For example, some of the very successful entrepreneurs in America have strong beliefs in empowerment when it comes to their ability to control outcomes. The general public, on the other hand, can be rather fatalistic, always blaming external forces that are out of their control, many waiting for the President to save their world.

The complexity of China's transformation increases the range of cultural beliefs. While it may be easy for a traditional Chinese businessperson to circle every scale on the right of the scales, the new reality has Chinese people embracing both traditional and Western values and beliefs, especially amongst the younger generation in major cities. As we move through the next sections, consider how each of these beliefs plays a contextual role in every dimension of business, whether you're working to establish a business or market a business. Moving away from simple duality will help you strengthen the depths of your relationships in China. When you develop the skills to balance multiple beliefs in different dimensions, you will be a grounded business leader with ample success.

NOTES

1. Ming-Jer Chen, *Inside Chinese Business: A Guide for Managers Worldwide* (Boston: Harvard Business Press, 2001).
2. David Wallechinsky and Irving Wallace, "Origins of Sayings—When in Rome, Do As the Romans Do." http://www.trivia-library.com/b/origins-of-sayings-when-in-rome-do-as-the-romans-do (accessed March 15, 2009).
3. Carl G. Jung, *The Undiscovered Self* (New York: Penguin Group Inc., 1958).

RELATIONAL CONSIDERATIONS
EVERY SECOND

Relationships are the center of Chinese culture. While the family is the basic operating unit, the connections between families define one's ability to live in harmony. This factor presents significant challenges to the reductionist approach, since it ignores the relationships between parts and only analyzes the parts that make up the whole. On the surface, many people in both the West and China believe in the importance of relationships. Underneath, however, the degree of importance is drastically different. Looking at a previous values study, Dr. Geert Hofstede found that the Chinese have the highest score in their long-term orientation, which leads towards a greater focus on relationships.[1] The Chinese had a score of 118, while many Western countries scored in the thirties, as did Germany, Australia, and the United States. The short-term orientation of the West steers behaviors towards immediate outcomes, while the long-term orientation of the Chinese guides behaviors to future rewards through the development of persistent relationships.

The Pursuit of Harmony

The focus on relationships has been a virtue in Chinese history for thousands of years. Confucian philosophy resides in one's ability to achieve harmony within the environment. This harmony required a peaceful existence within oneself and with others through relationships. As a consistent thread that was woven through China's philosophical journey, the value of an individual had two major constructs within harmony. First, knowledge of self came from the realization of one's unique contributions to society. Many of the philosophical foundations in Chinese history called for a moral existence that perpetuated inner peace (what Westerners call congruence). Such an existence compelled individuals to spend time reflecting on one's behaviors and decisions and their alignment with moral principles. As a result, the perspective of time is rather different in traditional Chinese cultures. Time spent on reflection and relationships is not about efficiency, as in the West. The reflective nature perceives time as a cyclical concept.

The second major construct within harmony is one's relationship to others. Traditional thought advocates relationships as a gradual movement of mutual understanding through dialogue and collaboration. With the long-term orientation towards most decisions, relationships are long-term ventures that require significant effort and often continue from generation to generation. This reality became evident while I was conducting my study. After having been away for over 25 years, living in the United States, many relationships were as strong as I remembered them to be.

A Powerful Web of "Old" Relationships

Consider for a second a good friendship you had 25 years ago, but one you haven't done much to maintain. If you were to ask for something from that person that required significant efforts, how would that person respond?

In Western society, relationships are relatively young due to the amount of movement available for many generations. Some people might be able to trace back friendships of their parents but are unlikely to be able to do so for friendships of their grandparents. The ability to move between regions created a young "relationship age." In Chinese culture, the limited movement between regions for many generations has developed relationships that are generations old. Compounded by the high value of relationships, one can have relationships passed down from one's grandparents. This was the case in my family. When I returned to teach leadership in a university and conduct research, my family was incredibly supportive. They extended their network of relationships without a second thought. While sharing for hours about the past experiences of old relationships between families, I realized the reach of relationships and its potential. In one conversation with my childhood playmate Iris, she extended her relationships of knowledgeable experts immediately. Within the next few hours, she had arranged meetings with them the next day. Compare that timeline with a typical Western introduction. If one makes an introduction, the meeting would typically happen in a week or longer, rarely in one single day.

The speed of powerful relationships drove me to explore further. Looking at the context of my relationship with her, Iris was my favorite playmate when I was young. She was the only person in my life that I've asked to marry me, at the age of eight! While I had no real concept of marriage, she innocently responded, "I can't marry you; it would not work; you're so tall and I'm so small." Since my departure at age ten, Iris and I had minimal contact until my visit in 2000. Recently, I've discovered that the connections are much deeper than my silly marriage proposal at eight years old. Both of our families knew each other for many decades. Iris's uncle and father both knew my father, and they played together in their childhood. Further investigation into the extent of relationships found that my step-grandfather in the United State was Iris's grandfather's cousin. So considering the many generations of connections, the importance of relationships weaves complex web of interconnectedness between people. With powerful relationships, many desired outcomes can happen quickly.

The power of these relationships is further quantified by an unexpected outcome in my study. The study of response time was not part of my initial thoughts. My web designer, Andrew Hippensteele, had the brilliance to track the dates of survey participation. As the email invitation went out requesting participation, I found a much longer lag between email request and completion of the survey in my Western contacts. It's rather fascinating to know that while my relationships are much more current in the West, they actually took more time to respond to the email request. As seen in table 4.1.1, the response time for Westerners was much longer than for those of Chinese business leaders. This outcome can lead to many more studies about relationships and time orientations. There are many factors that could have influenced this outcome, such as the perception of time. In Western society, it's the norm to do something for a friend when a perceived convenience exists. In Chinese society, the value of the friendship drives immediate responses to show respect. Within a very short amount of time, I was able to gather more responses from Chinese business leaders than from Western business leaders.

Even more interestingly, I had a few Western colleagues who had worked in China for a number of years. When one colleague sent the email request to his network, a few replied back that the survey was too long, indicating too much of an effort. The same request by Chinese people did not yield that response. This evidence illustrates the power of "old" relationships. The amount of effort had limited significance compared to the complex dimensions of relationships. This outcome suggests a major challenge to ponder— can Westerners really be competitive in the dimension of relationships with the Chinese who have generations of connectivity with each other?

Strategically, it would be wise to partner with a Chinese business leader who has a large family. Ideally, due to the family hierarchy, this individual is also the oldest male of the generation. Such a strategic position in the middle of the web of relationships could yield incredible efficiencies and access to many roadblocks in any business venture. Even with leaders with a powerful ability to build relationships, it will be an uphill battle against centuries-old relationships between families. Working smarter in relationships allows

Table 4.1.1. Average response time from email request for participation to survey participation.

	Chinese	Westerners
Average Response Time (days)	3.12	5.52

▰ MIND GEM 4.1 ▰

Mind Gem 4.1: When you arrive at a business meeting, how would you frame your mind for the meeting to be productive? The traditional Western culture may value efficiency and an objective flow of agenda items; the Chinese value the relational context as an important process for meetings as well. The following is a number of questions that will help set your mind in a healthy context that blends both perspectives.

Tactical steps:

Pre-Meeting Mental Framework

1. Allow your mind to flow as it is trained to do. Do not interrupt your mind's natural process that's gotten you to be successful at this point. You may be jotting down all of the agenda items that need to be discussed and some resolutions/ideas for improvement. This is the content that dominates meetings in Western business practices.

2. After letting your mind run naturally, it's time to frame the context of the meeting. Ask yourself the following questions:
   a. What are the relational goals for this meeting?

continued on page 133

business ventures to be successful quickly. Working harder alone will be a constant challenge.

Relationships in Business

Let's put this abstract knowledge to practice. Knowing the extent and importance of relationships, what would you do when you arrive at a business meeting? How would you behave with a list of items that needs attention? Take a few moments to jot down your strategies for accomplishment.

In Chinese business meetings, unique characteristics focus on the importance of relationships first. The tables may be small so that people can sit closer together with enough room on the table for tea. The closeness of seating minimizes the adversarial positioning around a large conference table. In order to preserve or further develop harmony, the context of collaboration influences attendees to spend a significant amount of time on what appears as small talk. In reality, the majority of the conversation at the start of meetings focuses on building relationships and seeking understanding. The last few minutes of the meeting revolves around the tangible agenda items.

In most business contexts, taking the time to build relationships is more important than an immediate need for resolution on issues. The conversations concerning personal well being contextually inform Chinese business leaders that you care about their lives. Moving rapidly forward into business topics can be seen as an uncaring gesture. I have found myself having to struggle with this at times. When writing emails on business issues with leaders, I tend to get right to the point quickly. The initial email is always tactical and very practical. Once that thought process is complete, I go back to the start of the email and enter the personal considerations that focus on the relationship. Asking about their personal well being and even family matters creates a context of care. It is that care in relationships that makes the difference between leaders and managers.

Generational Perspective

While all of the above discussions are true, they may not be the absolute "Truth." At senior levels of business and government, the older generation will have a heavy influence from traditional virtues of harmony and importance of relationships. At lower levels of many organizations, the younger generation may have a blend of both traditional philosophies and Western influences. They may practice some elements of the relational focus in some situations, but Western perspectives in others. For example, the traditional relationship hierarchy calls for a clear positional status. In some of the young, status is not a major factor in relationships. Materialism has taught many young people to value appearances and material goods over intangible relationships. Many have shifted from a propensity for large savings towards a short-term orientation for consumerism. The economic changes in China's transitioning economy make strategic choices challenging when it comes to relationships. The younger generations exist in the continuum between short- and long-term orientations and also between the importance of intangible relationships and tangible success factors. Like a child with his first taste of candy, the younger generation is enjoying the fruits of China's developments. In the long run, the maturation of this generation will lead towards a harmonious balance between China's traditions and Western influences.

A Trust Assessment

One key dimension of solid relationships is trust. In order to understand your ability to develop trust, consider the following simple assessment. The assessment is

continued from page 132

b. How can I establish the ideal emotional context of the meeting?

c. What is the relationship between/amongst the attendees and myself? Consider drawing a relational diagram in a hierarchical structure with position, age, and family considerations.

d. Connecting the content to context:

    i. What needs to be developed relationally for my agenda to be accomplished?

    ii. Which individual relationships are most important for each agenda item?

3. Before arriving at the meeting, consider the final framework question—how can I further the trust and respect through symbolic tactics?

Since emotions drive the majority of decisions in people, the Chinese people's attention to relationships simply create the emotional context. Attention to relationships may appear to be inefficient at the start; the work later is much smoother when relationships are solid.

like a camera, taking snapshots of intangible images of trust between you and another individual. You can start this learning process with your immediate team or friends if you like. Once you learn to apply it, take it with you to China to understand how trust may develop in relationships and how the Chinese business leaders may trust you. The process is a scientific exploration of specific strategies to develop trust. Ask a group to take the assessment concerning their level of trust with you. If you are comfortable with statistics, you can break down the results by gender, educational background, or length of relationship. If not, feel free to do an average of the ratings. This average will establish a baseline.

Once the baseline is complete, consciously create and execute a strategy to develop trust. While this may sound foreign, a conscious effort on building trust can yield profound results in all aspects of life. If you look at the amount of money trusted and respected brands charge compared to mediocre brands, it's obvious that trust yields higher outcomes. As an example, one strategy could be to stop using the word "try" in your vocabulary. When others hear the word "try," it's a weak statement with many possible connotations. Some may think you are going to make an effort; others may think you are giving them lip service to avoid hurt feelings. Either way, the use of the word does not further the relational trust element. Once you remove the

"Trust Assessment"

Statement	Disagree						Agree
1. I have a good friendship with this individual.	1......2......3......4......5......6......7						
2. I am able to count on this individual in times of need.	1......2......3......4......5......6......7						
3. I communicate well with this individual.	1......2......3......4......5......6......7						
4. I feel connected to this individual.	1......2......3......4......5......6......7						
5. I feel that the individual understands me.	1......2......3......4......5......6......7						
6. If I need a babysitter for my children, I would not hesitate in calling this individual for help.	1......2......3......4......5......6......7						
7. I feel a sense of responsibility toward this individual.	1......2......3......4......5......6......7						
8. I am excited to see this individual.	1......2......3......4......5......6......7						
9. I understand this individual.	1......2......3......4......5......6......7						
10. If my car breaks down, this individual would be one of the first people I'd call.	1......2......3......4......5......6......7						

word from your vocabulary, you'll also find that thought processes change. To make a firm commitment, thought around the achievement of an outcome is solidified by processes. On the surface, you'd be direct in sharing with people whether you'd achieve an outcome or not. As a result, it can quickly change how people see you and trust your word. I've had many executives implement this strategy with great success.

After a few months, measure the trust dimension once again with the same group of people. The results will provide you with a comparison between baseline and current levels of trust. One key aspect to keep in mind is that the new strategy is only one conscious effort. Many environmental influences can also move trust levels between people. Approaching life from an empowerment perspective, your conscious efforts to strategically improve trust as one ability will lead to greater likelihood of success in China.

THE TRUST ASSESSMENT

The individual of interest is _____. Ask a few colleagues or friends to complete the assessment. They will be answering all ten questions with regard to how they feel about you.

Upon collecting the results, enter them into an Excel spreadsheet and take a simple average. This becomes your baseline for future comparisons.

NOTE

1. Geert Hofstede, *Culture's Consequences: Comparing Values, Behaviors, Institutions, and Organizations across Nations*, 2nd ed. (Thousand Oaks, CA: Sage Publications, 2000).

Establishing Your Business

Starting a business in China is quite a different process from the Western world. Aside from the different legal framework, the establishment of relationships and interpretations of contracts provide a worthy challenge to many brilliant business leaders. In my study, one of my colleagues at SMC University (an international business university—Swiss Management Center, located in Switzerland and Austria) introduced to me his friend who was a successful American businessman with significant challenges in manufacturing products in China. We'll call this individual Marty. After analyzing his challenging experiences, it was clear that the majority of Marty's issues in product quality came from the business setup process.

Marty is an experienced businessman who sought to mass-market innovative products. His clients range from innovators to major marketers. His core business evolved around taking an inventor's product and mass-producing it in China. In most cases, the innovators have already received significant demand for the product. When asked about his experiences in doing business in China, his initial response was one of major frustration. "It's going to be a huge challenge for any Westerner attempting to have products made." Let's look at what led to this level of frustration.

Marty's first trip to China took him to a tradeshow where he felt lost. Even with a translator who attempted to communicate his needs, he knew the real message wasn't getting through. He realized that while some of the translations might be accurate, the conceptual ideas behind the words were quite different. For example, the concept of a cup in Western mentality could be a coffee cup or a glass for soda or water, so the cup is relatively large in size. In China, a cup is used for tea, so it is significantly smaller than a cup in Western society. While the word "cup" was the same, the relative size and usage was rather unique. That was the first challenge he faced. In other words, common terms or concepts that he thought were simple might have meant something very different to the

Chinese. Anything in manufacturing needed to be precise. The cultural barrier meant that communicating the idea of precision was very challenging.

As Marty gained experience, he decided to hire a local Chinese professional—a young woman in her mid-twenties we'll call Susie. Susie's role was to oversee the production of products and acquire suitable manufacturers for Marty's products. Marty was very specific on the exact details of the products, from type of material to tolerance of sizes. While the detailed specifications for products were clear on paper, the end result was different from the specifications. From Marty's perspective, the Chinese factories interpreted his design their own way. "There are nothing but problems with the factories. They can't understand my needs on quality and consistency, even with people I employ."

In this situation, Marty created the context of blame and placed fault with Chinese factories. This approach greatly limits Marty's own ability to resolve the problem, since he's not taking responsibility for these outcomes. Unfortunately, the context of Western business tends to have a strong influence of a "blaming" mentality. When something doesn't go right, many people point a finger at others. To fully understand the outcome of Marty's experiences, a few cultural highlights may shed some light on exactly how these events came about. Before reading on, can you identify the root causes for these outcomes? Many of these outcomes have a direct relation to the establishment of the business. To further understand some of the intricacies of a business startup, four major considerations set the proper foundation for success: linguistic and conceptual connotation, location selection, legal considerations, and partner relationships.

LINGUISTIC AND CONCEPTUAL CONNOTATION

Just as in the example of the cup, many words in the Western world may not reflect the same meaning in Chinese. Some commonly used words may even have negative connotations. For example, many Westerners freely use the word "globalization" to describe current economic events around the world. How might that simple word cause an issue? One of the challenges in China's history was the series of lost wars against foreign powers from 1840 through 1945. With over a century of colonial rule with many imposed economic and cultural sanctions, the Chinese have varying degrees of aversion to foreign businesspeople appearing as colonialists. When people use the word globalization, the emotionally loaded historical era loads the connotation negatively. Instead, the Chinese use the term "modernization."

Another major term is "business." In Western society, business is a set of transactional exchanges completed by some contract. In China, business has a strong tie to relationships. With a strong influence for achieving world harmony, the Chinese people focus on achieving solid long-term partners. Common practices, like blame from the West, appear to be elitist and also add shame to the relationship, which will terminate possibilities in most situations. Therefore, successful business interaction requires conscious understanding of the Chinese culture and its history.

"Negotiation" is another word that did not exist in the Chinese language. With a foundation of achieving harmony amongst each other, the Chinese prefer to simply talk. The influence of Western business practices has created a new term that defines negotiation—*tan pan*. "Tan" means discussion and "pan" means making a judgment. Ideally, the context of negotiation is a last resort. With business agreements, the majority of the conversations focus on building a relationship. Regardless of the content outcome of a business deal, the Chinese focus on the long-term relationship between people as another goal. As we move forward in this chapter, remember that the word negotiation signifies a Western approach. The equivalent Chinese concept ideally relates to further discussion and relationship building. I don't, therefore, recommend you even use the word "negatiation" when dealing with Chinese business partners.

From a linguistic perspective, many words in the English or other languages may not exist directly in the Chinese language. Common words like "computer," for example, use a combination of words that translate into "electronic brain." From a content perspective, you'd have to be a very experienced translator to know all of these differences and their various connotations from a historical and cultural perspective. As a contextual strategy, there's a very simple solution. With or without a translator, share the intent of a communication when communicating with Chinese. This tactic clearly illustrates the end point or goal of the communication. While helping to set the desired context for the conversation, it can also balance one's possible misuse of words. When inappropriate words appear, the clear intent allows the recipient to see the disconnect between the word (the content) and the clear intent of the communication (the context). Since the Chinese are usually interested in building long-term relationships, they will take the time to ask for clarification. This tactic can be a powerful contextual strategy when working with many cultures.

LOCATION SELECTION

As in any new business venture, the selection of a business location has the typical considerations such as infrastructure, environmental considerations, municipal friendliness, and worker availability. Especially in China, the drastic differences in educational level of workers from one region to another can create significant challenges. In most regions, building a factory may not be as challenging since there are millions of migrant laborers seeking work. Building a service business will require skilled workforce and managers. The selection of a region becomes more challenging due to the shortage of qualified and experienced managers.

Since China is still a developing country, the discrepancies in development provide major infrastructure challenges. Technology infrastructure in many major cities already exists. The rural areas may vary depending on the level of

MIND GEM 4.2

Mind Gem 4.2: When communicating with another culture, it's easy to get trapped in misunderstanding based on the misuse of words that have different connotations in various cultures. As a contextual strategy to mitigate this possibility, create the desired context for building a relationship by sharing the intent up front.

Tactical steps:

Creating a Desired Context

Start communications with the following options:

1. As a communication/meeting starts, ask for the goals: "What would you like to accomplish in this meeting?"
2. Share your perspective on the goals—this is the tangible part that many Western businesspeople are used to. You may also want to contextualize their stated goal with your goals to show commonality (a contextual goal).
3. Share your intentions on the desired contextual outcomes. From a relational perspective, this is a great challenge to consciously adopt: "My intent for our dialogue is . . . so that we can build better trust . . ." The focus of this

continued on page 141

development. Roads are another major consideration. Today, China has quite an extensive highway system to accommodate the needs of businesses and citizens. The one fascinating aspect about the people is that there is no shortage of potential. When government establishes a clear goal, the people will rally to make it happen. For example, how long does it take for your local government to make changes to a highway, like adding an extra lane for a few miles/kilometers? In the United States, it's common to see a road construction project extend for several years with rarely visible workers. And this is only for an upgrade. When China realized the need for a highway (an outer belt going around the city of Shanghai), they built it in two years. Even more impressive, due to the incredible density of the city, there was no land to build a highway. So they built it above ground-level. Imagine the amount of work required to build a highway above ground surrounding one of the largest and most populated cities in the world. Recently, China built the incredible structure called the Bird's Nest for the 2008 Olympics in a matter of a few years. With this in mind, the potential of establishing infrastructure is tremendous. The major caveat is the degree of commitment and strength of relationships you have with local and regional authorities.

LEGAL CONSIDERATIONS

The legal aspects of doing business in China are rather complex. Unlike many developed Western societies, China is still in the process of developing its legal framework. Within this developing context, there are two major challenges: establishment of the business and legal compliance. To obtain permission from the government for business ventures, a number of hurdles present complex challenges that call for ample patience. From a government perspective, one may be able to get the paperwork completed in Western societies in a matter of months; ventures in China may take anywhere from six months to multiple years for final approval depending on the scale of investment. If the venture is under $10 million, local authority can make approval relatively simple. Ventures larger than $10 million require provincial approval. The Ministry of Foreign Trade and Economic Cooperation (MOFTEC) will add another layer of complexity for ventures above $30 million.[1] With the involvement of multiple layers, the hierarchically structured bureaucracy can be slow in expediting approval for a business venture. One of the possible causes is that the different levels of authorities may be uncooperative in the midst of political gains in the constantly changing environment. Permissions from one entity will challenge people to obtain many stamps of approval at various levels.

The typical process for approval starts off with a letter of intent. Depending on the volume of investment, an appropriate authority approves it to move towards a feasibility study. The applicant then has to produce a detailed project description that covers three major parts: technical characteristics, economic-legal compliance, and socioeconomic considerations. The technical portion of the study focuses on the products, production requirements, facilities, procedures, and raw materials. The economic-legal portion quantifies the legal form of the organization, market and risk analysis, possible political influence from parent company, and profit-loss projects. The final aspect of socioeconomic considerations encompasses the environmental concerns of the location and necessary infrastructure. After the feasibility study is completed and approved, the governing authority can require further amendments, if necessary, before approval.[1] Furthermore, depending on the business type, other agencies are also involved. For example, if you are a construction firm, Decree No. 113, Regulations on Administration of Foreign Investment Construction Enterprises, calls for six additional steps to acquire a construction license.[2]

Aside from the due process for obtaining approval, the second major challenge facing foreign business ventures is compliance with what appears to be infinite laws and regulations. To make the challenge more difficult, regulatory bodies constantly create new regulations and laws. For many companies, these new laws can be a significant headache. For example, one firm was 50 percent complete with an approved construction project. A new regulation

continued from page 140

creates a contextual long-term goal that focuses on the relational aspect. Feel free to authentically state the intentions as you see fit, keeping in mind that the separation of personal and business is very limited in other cultures. Business is not just business. In relational and long-term oriented cultures like the Chinese, sharing the intent up front minimizes the speculation of intent by Chinese leaders based on content words, which will be problematic.

required additional changes to the basic materials of tempered glass. Regardless of the previous approval and the 50 percent completion, compliance was the only choice. This meant a significant rework of the entire project.[2]

While the formal aspect of the legal system may appear to be a significant challenge, there is another aspect which can be flexible and efficient. While laws and regulations are present to govern business, the Chinese tend to see regulations with a healthy flexibility. Imagine the strength of a fishing pole—its isotropic strength offers significant power along the pole. It is able to withstand great pressures pushing along the same axis as the pole. At the same time, it is incredibly pliable when it comes to torque or bending forces. These properties are similar for the regulations in China. When attempting to push it along the same axis of its many layers of approval, the time and effort is significant. For someone who knows how to work the system, it can be rather simple to bend the pole and reach the end point much faster. Depending on the regional authorities and one's depth and reach of relationships in the area, obtaining the stamps of approval can be relatively efficient.

So rather than working extremely hard in attempting to follow every step meticulously, one can choose to work smarter in the legal system and leverage relationships. The system of relationships is very flexible and ethically challenging. While one can be smart about creating powerful relationships, the balance lies with ethical considerations of knowing when it is too much. For many experienced foreign business leaders, relationship-based strategies provide an effective means to getting through the legal system. This leads us to finding business partners and building a strong foundation of social relationships.

PARTNER RELATIONSHIPS

Being in a different country, attempting to push your way through the legal jungle on your own would be akin to a bull running in a jewelry store. China offers many gems and shining opportunities; without a partner to get you through the cultural and legal challenges, success can be very costly and time consuming. Even if you've found the ideal location for the venture, a poor partner is a huge blunder. When finding a partner, the typical Western approach may focus greatly on the technical side—such as the use of resumes, technical capabilities, resource availability, management skills, financial health, and market knowledge. When an individual or organization embodies the technical side, it doesn't mean success.

Going back to Marty's situation, Susie had a good technical background. This was one of Marty's major downfalls in his selection of Susie as a Chinese counterpart for his business. While Susie may have had many of the skills and abilities, the relationship side was much more important. Susie was a young female, which created inherent challenges. What was completely unknown was the depth of her relationship network. Size of family is part of the value that one may bring to a foreign business. Being a female could also have its challenges as well within traditional Chinese gender roles.

Within this area of relationships, there's more than one dimension. There's the first dimension of relationship between the foreign investor or businessperson and the Chinese partner. We'll discuss that part later. The first consideration of a solid partner is the second dimension of relationship—the partner's network of relationships. As you're looking for a business partner, the organization should have individuals who have an extensive network that opens doors at many levels of government and with key families. Since direct communication with Chinese government officials may be difficult and not too helpful, the partner's access to high-ranking officials enables the flexibility of legal process. A full assessment of the partner's network of relationship is the first task.

This was one of the major flaws in Marty's approach. While he had trust in Susie's abilities as a manager, he had no idea of what type of networks she possessed. Further inquiries concerning the selection of factories for the parts led to more evidence of a poor network. Since it was Susie's responsibility to acquire the best factory, the outcome was indicative of a lack of relationship between Susie and the factory. Two additional factors may have influenced the depth of relationship—Susie's youth and gender. As someone in their mid-twenties, her connections with older, senior-level executives and officials were limited. Being a female also presented some challenges on the relational side. If Marty was to acquire consistent quality products, one strategic choice on a local presence would lead to an individual who had solid relationships with senior-level executives and officials.

BUILDING THE PARTNER RELATIONSHIP

Once you've identified the partner, the first dimension of a relationship with the potential partner can be longer than the Western norm. While the West tends to conduct business with contracts and financial agreements, China requires a very different approach. The establishment of a relationship based on trust and respect is the starting point for any major business venture. The Chinese tend to spend a significant amount of time on "small talk" to get to know you. Depending on the size of the venture, it would be wise to invite the potential partner to your country. However, be very careful if you take this approach. When the Chinese are visiting you in your home city, they will be assessing your network of relationships as well. They may strategically ask for uncommon options that would require the assistance of your extended network. This action seeks to assess the strength of your relationships. If all goes well, the hospitality would be returned in China.

In China, building relationships is just that. There is no separation between business and personal as there is in many Western societies. From a holistic perspective, the Chinese take a long-term approach and desire to see the complete "you" living in harmony. This relational objective may take time, with many dinners, karaoke sessions, and social gifts. Two specific characteristics exist in building these types of relationships. First, many

Westerners often focus on understanding the differences in cultures. When building relationships with the Chinese, the focus resides in establishing common ground, not finding differences. The myth of seeking differences can often separate cultures even further.

The second characteristic concerns gift giving for social reasons. In one study, researchers found that 68 percent of small businesses sent social gifts to key individuals.[3] Another study also found that gift giving is a widely accepted and legal practice in China.[4] While I was in China during late October, crab season had just reached its peak. During this season, countless urban residents travel to the rural areas to enjoy the crabs from the farms. While having lunch at one of the crab farms, I witnessed one individual making a 30,000 RBM (approximately 4,300 USD or 3,500 EUR) purchase of crabs that completely filled a minivan. Each box or two was a social gift towards stakeholders within his network. As he was making the purchase, he personally inspected a number of the boxes to make sure that the crabs were large and healthy. Such gifts are not rare in China. Since relationships are a major aspect of business, people spend significant effort and attention on meaningful gifts.

In assessing Western practice, it's clear that many gifts from companies tend to be generic and driven by a few holidays. The attention to relationships is minimal due to the strong influence of management principles, which ignore emotional content. From this perspective, Western eyes tend to make a judgment of ethics (i.e. "If we don't do it, it must be wrong"). The contextual message received by the Chinese is an elitist perspective that is perceived to be an attempt to change China. So as you're looking to create powerful relationships to work for you, the major challenge is balancing Western approaches with Chinese practices without judgment. Without breaking your code of ethics, build relationships that are meaningful. It doesn't always require a significant amount of funds to give lavish gifts. Being thoughtful in meaningful gifts can also extend to family. Showing proper respect and taking people seriously can earn you much relational income.

CONTRACTS AND NEGOTIATIONS

Once you've built a strong relational foundation with the potential partner, it's time to create a contract. From the Western perspective, a contract is a binding document that clearly outlines all expectations of the business transaction. For the Chinese, the actual words are not as rigid even though they may negotiate intensely on them. The symbolic nature in the spirit of the contract is more important than the actual words. So be very cautious about your approach to contracts in any Chinese business venture. The specifics of contracts do not rule the Chinese; instead, a relationship of mutual understanding is the foundation of contracts.

When planning for negotiations, a pre- and post-negotiation framework has relational significance. Especially with possible sensitive topics, the attention on the pre- and post-negotiations tends to take the edge off the actual content. Being a culture of harmony, the Chinese are not willing to drive conflicts toward a resentful end. As a general rule, meeting halfway will show significant respect for the relationship. Thanks to Confucian influences, contractual procedures and legal requirements of the West are not as important as one's self-image or face (*mianzi* in Chinese). The pre- and post-negotiation activities ensure a solid societal relationship. As long as the efforts to build a trusting relationship exist early in the process, the contract negotiations (talks) will be relatively smooth.

As for the detailed content of the contract, here are some general rules that are unique to the Chinese culture:

- General agreement enables details to fall in place. There is no need to be too detailed.
- The contract has symbolic importance, while the details are to be continuously interpreted.
- If you make a concession of anything, ask for something in return. This doesn't need to be anything significant. The contextual message is to be fair and equal in the partnership.
- Finally, do not push detailed commitments too early. This can mean the end to a relationship as it contextually eliminates the continued efforts for trust.

ESTABLISHING YOUR MENTAL CONTEXT

While the content of the above information is rather profound, the contextual framework within a new venture in China offers incredible perspectives that many Western business leaders would benefit from. At least for another decade, starting a business in China without a partner is very challenging, especially if you wish to build any kind of significant enterprise. Learn to work smarter, rather than harder. Once you tap into the existing networks of powerful relationships, the potential is incredible. Two questions to frame your mental context as you start the journey:

1. How would I incorporate a long-term perspective in every dimension of business?
2. How am I focusing on relationships and achieving harmony with others?

The questions above are not intended to be simple. The words within each question embody both a historical and philosophical value basis. Tactically, you can break each question down to major themes such as "What is a long-term perspective?" and "What are the dimensions of business?" You can come up with major themes for discovery in the second question. For each exploration, provide yourself ample time to find and understand information on the topic. More importantly, experience it when you arrive in China. All theoretical knowledge has limited value if you don't have the skills to perceive situations holistically.

NOTES

1. Birgit Zinzius, *Doing Business in the New China: A Handbook and Guide* (Westport, CT: Praeger, 2004).
2. Florence Yean Yng Ling and Sook Ping Low, "Legal Risks Faced by Foreign Architectural, Engineering, and Construction Firms in China," *Journal of Professional Engineering Education and Practice* 133(3) (July 2007): 239–40.
3. Thomas Leung and L. L. Yeung, "Negotiation in the People's Republic of China: Results of a Survey of Small Business in Hong Kong," *Journal of Small Business Management* 33(1) (1995): 73.
4. Qing Tian, "Perception of Business Bribery in China: The Impact of Moral Philosophy," *Journal of Business Ethics* 80(3) (July 2008): 437–45.

PRODUCT AND MARKET WISDOM

No money can be made without a solid marketing plan. This specific chapter focuses on a product or service that you intend to market within the Chinese marketplace. With a population of over 1.3 billion, the potentials appear to be rather significant. Unfortunately, that is only a surface view. Looking deeper, the disparities in socioeconomic status make the marketing aspect much more complex. One major advantage to the Chinese market is the high concentration of the Chinese population residing in eastern provinces. Furthermore, the relatively young age of its consumers provides a sustainable revenue source, if a firm is capable of high customer retention.

Within the field of marketing, many challenges exist in current literature and practices. While a marketing mix such as the 4 P's (product, pricing, placement, and promotion) are commonly used in Western organizations, some of the major challenges in marketing rest in analyzing the information behind the numbers in marketing research and accurately measuring the relationship between a specific marketing strategy and organizational performance or customer value. While there are ample studies on Western marketing strategies and processes, studies surrounding Chinese markets are starting to develop.

STRATEGIC CHOICES—WHAT TO BE?

One of the first choices in marketing a product or service is to determine the entry level. The overall Chinese market has a thirst for new products from the outside. Yet, the level of income is often prohibitive for many firms to enter with their normal pricing and marketing strategies. You can choose to be a market leader introducing new products and services. While this could be a great market position, it can also be costly to establish initial brand image. Being a market follower may minimize the initial marketing costs to build product or service awareness. One major challenge in taking this position is the likelihood that someone else in China has already done it at a cheaper rate. Being an incredibly adaptive culture, many new products and services are often reengineered and produced at a lower cost. Strategic position as a market follower will open you to the possibility of numerous competitors in many regional/local levels.

Another strategic choice for products and services is to focus on a niche. The beauty of niche marketing is the high profitability with a specific focus on a specific segment. Looking at the demographics of China, there are many luxury firms in China, such as Gucci, BMW, and Bentley, targeting the wealthy. Their focus is on a very small niche with such access to funds to enjoy luxury goods. Interestingly enough, if you desire such products, buying them from China will cost you at least 10 percent more compared to prices in many Western nations. The demand for high-end products in this particular niche allows the vendors to charge more for these products. A significant market of interest is the increasing middle class. As in the United States, this market represents a significant portion of the consumers with money to spend. Unlike in the United States, this class is increasing with tremendous potential in China. Especially with a youthful generation, this market has embraced many Western principles such as a higher rate of consumption and lower rate of savings.

DISPELLING A MAJOR MYTH: HOMOGENOUS TO MARKET SEGMENTATION

China is much more complex than one single homogenous population. Especially from a marketing perspective, the desires and capabilities of the various markets are incredibly diverse. For example, over 400 million Chinese live on less than two dollars per day. How does that influence marketing choices? Along with a combination of unique local cultures, each local market may have its unique values, beliefs, traditions, language (dialect), and customs. Furthermore, regional differences such as those between Beijing and Shanghai are drastic when it comes to fashion and tastes.[1,2] With a large percentage of the rural population lagging behind many urban centers, market segmentation and your ability to accurately identify the market is crucial to success.

When looking at market factors, demographic variables include economic development of a region, socioeconomic status of the population, local cultures, generational uniqueness, gender preferences, and each group's values and beliefs. These factors drive consumer demand. Organizations cannot simply rely on market research data which, if it exists, can be temperamental. Creating a mechanism to uniquely assess the demands of a market on a specific segment will provide the most accurate data.[3]

SUNGLASSES: A GOLDEN OPPORTUNITY

Moving forward, let's take the tremendous opportunity in providing sunglasses as an example that many Westerners can understand. In Western societies, it's not rare for individuals to have more than one pair of sunglasses. Some people have specialized sunglasses for different sports such as bike riding or volleyball. In China, the use of sunglasses is relatively low. This was one of my most fascinating realizations when I arrived in China and had forgotten my sunglasses. Being used to using them, I found it tough to do all of the walking in Shanghai and Beijing without them. As I searched around to find a comfortable pair, it took a bit more effort than in the United States, where there are sunglasses shops all over the malls and on corners of streets. So if you're one of the first to read this book, take a look at the potential of the sunglasses market. With a population of 1.3 billion, the majority does not have a pair. You can be a first mover to truly establish this market.

Now that we've got a product possibility, let's look at the various markets you may explore. We'll only take the perspective of socioeconomic status as an example here, with a hint of some other influences. If we were to apply all of the factors for market segmentation, it would be an entire book. The processes of consideration for each of the factors are consistent when you chose to apply them for your product.

At the top level, about five to ten percent have a significant wealth.[4] The majority of these people live in major cities such as Shanghai, Beijing, and Hong Kong. This market has had ample research and desires the latest in fashion from the West. Going into three major cities may also be challenging. A strategic starting point could be with Shanghai, as that population is much more fashion-conscious. You could easily start promoting top brands such as Oakley, Ray-Ban, and Gucci, with a focus on each individual having more than one pair for different activities such as shopping or playing golf.

The middle and lower class represent the majority of China's population with drastic differences. The great aspect about sunglasses as a product is that the pricing can vary greatly according to market demands. This is one of the reasons I chose sunglasses as an example, aside from the incredible potential it offers. While the profit margins may be lower, the middle-class market has an undiscovered taste for sunglasses as a fashion. When I finally found a store that sold sunglasses in a shopping mall, they only had two to three styles for males (I could not believe the lack of selection, especially considering the low inventory cost). The higher end was Ray-Ban with a lower end by a local company. The salesperson did not ask many obvious questions such as the purpose of the sunglasses or my frequency of use. The lack of knowledge in the application of sunglasses further illuminates the possibilities of this product. Imagine the education that a knowledgeable salesperson can easily achieve with a middle-class consumer—the middle-class consumer often has a few hobbies besides eating and working. Once a salesperson understands the various hobbies of the customer, they can easily provide fashionable and health-oriented information on appropriate sunglasses for these hobbies. Considering that health is many Chinese people's top value, the conversion rate for the sale would increase drastically with its inclusion in the sales process.

Going down to the lowest level of income (those who may live on less than two dollars per day), it still represents over 400 million potential consumers. Many of these consumers are laborers who spend a great deal of time outside in the sun. Just as in the United States, cheap sunglasses offer the low income some sense of fashion and protection from the sun. As a nation of active learners, education would be a key driver to create such a demand. This market would not be as profitable and easy since they are more diversely populated across the country.

The age of specific markets can also play a significant role. Since younger consumers are much more fashion oriented with a bias toward foreign brands, they can be a great target within a class segment.[5] The symbolism of wearing popular foreign brands can drive up prices, making it more profitable. Using the existing desire for top brands, major sunglasses firms or distributors can leverage this desire for optimal profitability.

The existing data for further analysis is still very limited. Market data such as consumer behavior based on educational level, marital status, and occupation is very limited. Looking at the overall data on market segmentation, it would be wise to focus on developing the sunglasses product line according to style, workmanship, color, and brand. The starting market for maximum profitability would be the younger generations within the middle class in Shanghai. These consumers have disposable income with a great sense of fashion compared to other regions.[1,2] Guangzhou and Beijing would be the next two target markets. The greatest and most interesting challenge is creating a promotional campaign to fit the values and beliefs of the specific market segment. Creating an undiscovered need amongst millions has already been done by many foreign firms.

BASIC MARKETING FRAMEWORK APPLIED—THE 4 P's

The conventional perspective of a marketing mix typically focuses on four basic elements called the 4 P's: product, price, place, and promotion. Application of this approach in China has its unique twists that may surprise you. We'll continue to use the sunglasses example where applicable to illustrate some of the fascinating aspects of the Chinese marketplace.

PRODUCT

The first consideration of marketing rests with the product or service and how it meets customers' desires and needs. A mistake that some Western businesspeople tend to make is the blind application of proven methods in Western societies. Due to the developing nature of the country, along with unique values and beliefs that form culture, the consumers' desires and needs for a product or service may be very different. Before looking to bring a product to China, one should take the time to balance the historical success in Western societies with the desires and needs of the Chinese consumer.

For example, Western societies such as the United States enjoy ample space in their homes and roads. Unlike the European trading partners, this space provides room for large appliances and vehicles. China is an amazing, transforming environment. In the past, people were living in shacks with very small spaces and countless people filling up every street. Selling appliances that were space conscious was optimal for logical reasons. Yet, the transition of the economy has begun to witness larger homes for many people as the construction of homes began to rise. Rather than fitting 100 people into a specific living space in a few floors of a building, today's living space can house thousands in the same space. The high-rise apartments in China are allowing some people to have ample space in their homes. So depending on the market segment, there may be some room for larger appliances. The market is still in major transition as many cities are still looking to replace many smaller living quarters with large apartment-style high-rise buildings.

The most important aspect to a product or service is the ability to meet or exceed the consumers' desires and needs. In order to achieve this, the crucial step is to fully understand the values and beliefs that drive consumer behavior. Understanding that health is the top value across many cities, generational gaps, and genders, many products and services have successfully been introduced. For example, many Chinese have practiced Tai Chi for centuries; yet in the pursuit of better health, the Chinese looked to other methods popular in the West. Yoga has been proven to provide relief for the increased stress of the workplace. Since 2005, it has been gaining popularity amongst many young people. These yoga studios are rather expensive, compared to the Western approaches. Many of the studios run by a monthly fee, rather than a per-class fee. Surprisingly, the monthly fee is similar to what many American studios charge, except people are doing it on a Chinese salary, which tends to be significantly less. This product has a specific appeal to an upper-middle-class market for health.

Another fascinating product that's been introduced in China recently is golf. When I was in China in 2000, the sport hadn't quite caught the wave. By 2008, it had become a very popular and expensive adult sport for many executives. Once again, the target market here is the upper to upper-middle class. I found it incredibly shocking to see golf clubs and driving ranges fitted into Shanghai—a city of around 20 million people. This is a city where people are stacked on top of each other every day with very limited development space. Yet, with powerful marketing, the product/service of golf has permeated the culture to an extent I thought would have been impossible. Today's golf resorts in China are extravagant, with many business and leisure services

■ MIND GEM 4.3 ■

Mind Gem 4.3: The many trends in China offer systemic products that will be needed for generations to come. Learning how to see the major coming trends and needs of the Chinese people will bear endless fruit for any organization. This level of thinking goes well beyond a single product or service. Seeing the entire system at work, from government policies to cultural trends, a developing nation offers incredible systemic opportunities.

Tactical steps:

1. Take some time to see the major drivers that the country is shifting towards.
   a. For example, due to the high population and food challenges before the 1980s, many Chinese diets were composed mostly of fruits and vegetables. This high limitation of meat products provided China with a degree of health. The current diet trend in China is like a child going into the candy store for the first time. The abundance of meat has many people shifting their diet

continued on page 153

allied to the sport/venue. Some even boast a bowling alley along with its fitness center.

From a service perspective, the abundance of cheap labor still makes China one of the most attractive business opportunities in the world. With an increasing need for high-quality service, millions of migrant workers provide ample basic services such as massage and beauty care. In Shanghai, I enjoyed many forms of massage from migrant workers who often work seven days a week. Their work ethic is naturally incredibly high, without exposure to many Western beliefs about work-life balance. They constantly focus on making more money to bring back home to their families in rural areas.

From a product or service perspective, a solid understanding of the many market segments in various parts of China provides a starting point for consideration. Knowing where to obtain cheap, quality resources is another crucial aspect to success. You might also consider the systemic offerings; they can return tremendous rewards that can shape an entire industry. For example, think of the Western medical system. Its powerful marketing engine created a population that cannot live without it. The drug companies provide the products and the doctors provide the service. Both form a system that provides an endless stream of consumers. Another example is the waste-hauling industry. Waste Management Inc., for example, used very aggressive strategies to acquire a significant share of the waste market. Today, the company has over $6 billion in annual sales. With a developing country like China, it pays to look at systemic opportunities. This is where empires of business begin.

PRICING

The challenge of price is more complex in China than in developed nations, where you may have a relatively stable income range.

Since China has such a diverse population, price setting can be rather challenging. For example, food is one of the cheapest delights in China. Yet, name-brand clothing is more expensive than in other parts of the world. Then there's also the challenge of fake products that dilute one's ability to always command a high price. If you set the price too high, it invites counterfeiters to copy your product and capture a lower market segment. The price is tightly connected to the specific market segment. Some segments of the market focus on price as a selling point; others focus on quality or aesthetics.[6]

Depending on the city, you may want to be very cautious of the target market. For example, is your target market the 5 million plus migrant workers in Shanghai, or the increasing middle class, or perhaps the top 5 to 10 percent of the upper class in Shanghai? Each segment requires different pricing models with consideration for relationships. If a product has a perceived equitable price, the power of word-of-mouth within the network of relationships can drastically increase demand overnight. The same is true if you price the product too high. With some products like sunglasses, the pricing can vary dramatically depending on the target market. With the disparity of income, you can easily price one model or brand of sunglasses for the upper class, one brand for the middle class, and one for the migrant workers. With the changing dynamics in China, being flexible with pricing gives you a tremendous advantage over competitors.

PLACEMENT

The placement of products refers to the means by which consumers acquire your products and services. Traditionally, retailing has dominated the Chinese marketplace. With dramatic advancements in technology, the Internet has completely changed product

continued from page 152

towards endless meat consumption.

b. Another example is the increasing amount of cars and drivers on the roads. With the incredible pace that China has built its modern highway system, driving personal vehicles is just over a decade old. This placed many inexperienced drivers on the road.

2. Compare these trends with traditional ways of life.

a. With the dramatic increase of meat intake, the general health of the Chinese is starting to show signs that are of concern. In the old days, it would be rare to find a "fat" Chinese. Today, there are many overweight kids and adults. Especially with increasing efforts at work or school to compete on a global level, the lack of exercise and abundance of meat are starting to build a tidal wave of health concerns, much like those faced by many Western countries.

b. When there was an abundance of bicycles and

continued on page 154

continued from page 153

busses that carried people from place to place, being hit by a bicycle wasn't too serious. Bus drivers also had years of experience to avoid major accidents. Today, the abundance of personal vehicles and taxis has completely changed the landscape in many cities.

3. Capitalize on the coming tidal wave of business.
   a. Health services that may steer the Chinese towards a different direction in health will be a major industry. Especially with a top value of health, the realization of the relationship between diet and health will offer many systemic product opportunities.
   b. The system of vehicles comes with many systemic products surrounding safety and education. Products like insurance can be quite lucrative with a high population.

placement. China had about 162 million Internet users in 2007, compared to 185 million in America. Currently, China has already begun to overtake the United States in Internet usage.[7] This trend provides significant opportunities for organizations to provide ample access to products and services via the Internet. Internet access is ideal for firms looking to reach the youth and 1980ers who are actively surfing the Web. While their disposable income is limited, the cost of customer acquisition may be significantly lower.

The traditional sense of place is still extremely important in the Chinese marketplace. The growing middle class with disposable income still does a large amount of walking. Due to limited space, even if people own a car, they'd still have to walk a distance to get to their destinations. This provides retailers ample consideration for window shopping. These window displays can help establish trends for the fashionable in Shanghai and Guangzhou.[8] Especially in such large cities where people walking on the streets offer endless marketing for your products and services, having a strategic placement in a busy intersection can yield great product launches.

PROMOTION

The final P is promotion. The typical means of promotion includes publicity, personal selling, advertising, and branding. One vital aspect that is unique to the Chinese marketplace is relationship marketing. In order to promote products successfully, the long-term perspective of relationship building is a conscious and strategic choice for those who wish to remain successful within their community. This type of promotion involves long-term activities that continue to enhance relationships with customers. Some theorists at the City University of Hong Kong's research center further quantified four key elements to relationship marketing including bonding, empathy, reciprocity, and trust.[9] The promotional aspect of these elements connects back to the many relationship aspects of the Chinese culture discussed in previous chapters.

Branding is also a crucial consideration. As with many Western brands, the perceived value of products and services influences buying decisions. In China, that perception also has a national bias towards foreign manufactures such as the USA and EU (developed countries).[10] Another fascinating aspect of branding that's unique to the Chinese culture is superstition. Certain numbers and names of businesses carry specific levels of superstition. Although the Chinese people are not religious, favorable numbers can be valuable assets. For example, the number 4 is like the unlucky number 13. Due to its pronunciation that's almost identical to the word for death, many Chinese people and businesses will avoid living or working in an address with the number 4. Other numbers of luck are 8 and 6.[11] There was a very important aspect to the start of the 2008 Olympics—it was on 08/08/2008 at 8 o'clock. All the eights attempted to bring fortune to the event. The superstition of the Chinese people is very interesting. You'll often find large shrines of gods in business owners' offices. While most people are not necessarily religious by Western standards, these owners will visit a temple during New Year's Eve to pay their respects.

With a high level of bias towards Western brands and fashion, using Western celebrities or sports stars can be a powerful promotional tool. If you have a desire to make a powerful sunglasses trend in China, have the U.S. basketball star Yao Ming, for example, pose for a poster-ad to initiate the trend. Yao's popularity is like that of Michael Jordan in the West. His Chinese heritage and Western fame make him a highly preferred marketing giant. Many non-existent trends have started in China since the start of the modernization efforts. Studying these creators of trends such as colored hair and golf can highlight a strategic path to making sunglasses a powerful business. Especially considering the shape of sunglasses is a horizontal 8, you can possibly capitalize on the superstition of wearing a lucky number in the Chinese market with some creative promotional ideas.

DEVELOPING A LONG-TERM PERSPECTIVE

China is undoubtedly an incredible marketplace for many organizations. Its vast and often inexpensive resources offer low-cost production. Its consumers are gaining wealth and disposable income at many levels along with a high sense of fashion amongst the young. Along with its economic development, China's marketplace has many organizations looking to tap into that abundance of potential. Still tied greatly to the importance of relationships, most people will want to work for successful companies that are innovative with great customer relationships. Since news travels fast within a tight network of relationships, people will be honored to be part of a respected company. This leads towards a long-term orientation. Studies have shown that many successful companies tend to have effective strategies in marketing that focus on the long term, rather than on short term gains.[12]

So as you consider marketing sunglasses or any other product into China, be very conscious of the market segmentation and the various unique aspects of the Chinese marketplace. Working with Chinese partners is often the first step. Balancing one's own experiences with new research needed for most ventures will be a crucial skill for long-term success. And when you learn the keys to successful marketing in China along with skills to build powerful partnerships, enormous success will be in your hands.

NOTES

1. Zhiming Zhang, Yi Li, Chen Gong, and Haidong Wu, "Casual Wear Product Attributes: A Chinese Consumers' Perspective," *Journal of Fashion Marketing and Management* 6 (2002): 53–62.
2. Ran Wei and Zhongdang Pan, "Mass Media and Consumerist Values in the People's Republic of China," *International Journal of Public Opinion Research* 11 (1999): 75–96.
3. Thomas Fischer, Heiko Gebauer, and Elgar Fleisch, "Redefining Product Strategies in China: Overcoming Barriers to Enter the Medium Market Segment," *Strategic Direction* 24 (2008): 3–5.
4. Emerald Group Publishing Limited, "Selling to China's Rich and Not So Rich: Need to Go Beyond the Luxury Market," *Strategic Direction* 21 (2005): 5–7.
5. Marsha A. Dickson, Sharron J. Lennon, Catherine P. Montalto, Dong Shen, and Li Zhang, "Chinese Consumer Market Segments for Foreign Apparel," *Journal of Consumer Marketing* 21 (2004).
6. Geng Cui, "Segmenting China's Consumer Market: A Hybrid Approach," *Journal of International Consumer Marketing* 11 (1999): 55–76.
7. Rebecca A. Fannin, *Silicon Dragon: How China Is Winning the Tech Race* (New York: McGraw-Hill, 2007).
8. Geng Cui and Qiming Liu, "Regional Market Segments of China: Opportunities and Barriers in a Big Emerging Market," *Journal of Consumer Marketing* 17 (2000): 55–72.
9. Alan C.B. Tse, Leo Y.M. Sin, Oliver H.M. Yau, Jenny S.Y. Lee, and Raymond Chow, "A Firm's Role in the Marketplace and the Relative Importance of Market Orientation and Relationship Marketing Orientation," *European Journal of Marketing* 38 (2004): 1158–72.
10. Sadrudin A. Ahmed and Alain d'Astous, *Consumer Behavior in Asia: Issues and Marketing Practice* (New York: Haworth Press, 1999).

11. Yi S. Ellis and Bryan D. Ellis, *101 Stories for Foreigners to Understand Chinese People* (Shenyang, China: Liaoning Education Press, 2007).
12. Wai-Sum Siu and Liu Zhi Chao, "Marketing in Chinese Small and Medium Enterprises (SMEs): The State of the Art in a Chinese Socialist Economy," *Small Business Economics* 25 (2005): 333–46.

CHAPTER 5

21ST CENTURY MULTINATIONAL BELIEFS AND SKILLS

The 20th century brought significant power and wealth to many Western societies. Along with those successes, certain rules of life played a crucial part. Unfortunately, as the world becomes smaller through technology and global business, many of those rules of life are no longer applicable. The greatest challenge facing many leaders is one's ability to see those rules that contain one's thoughts. Imagine yourself as a driver in a car racing for business success. After being inside the car for a century, you've won many races. Unfortunately, the new race requires you to see the outside of the vehicle as well as the inside of the engine. Being inside the car, you can't see the full exterior of the vehicle. In order to understand the new race of global business context like China does, getting outside of the car allows you to examine the new road of business and design a new vehicle that will win future races.

The following are some basic challenges that help leaders reflect on their perceptions and critically assess their rules for life. In order to be successful in China or in any other foreign country, reevaluating basic beliefs built on Western principles opens your mind for further exploration of alternative perspectives. Along with these reflective thoughts, China's unique culture plays a significant role in helping you shift your thinking process.

Ethics of Judgment

Is it moral to make judgments about another culture or people based on your values and beliefs? Theoretically most people would agree that we don't have a right to judge others, since we don't have a full picture of what these individuals experience from their perspectives. In reality, judgments are the norm. If someone cuts you off while driving, labels such as "idiot" or "jerk" may fly out of your mouth. In the workplace, when someone doesn't do their job with a certain quality or timeliness, they're labeled as being lazy or incapable. The fast-paced business environment often leads people towards hasty labels that blame people.

As I'm writing about this topic, I need to be conscious not to label certain groups as well. Otherwise, I'd be a hypocrite challenging people not to make judgments while doing it myself. The surface-level behavior that many Westerners have is judgment, which can be efficient at times for businesses. The deeper issue is the lack of critical thought driving a contextual system that greatly influences people to behave in a certain way.

This contextual system has two primary characteristics. First is the need to be efficient in all that we do. Since time, or the availability of it, is a significant challenge amongst many people, efficiency allows businesses to make more profits. We've all heard the common phrase "time is money." Quick decisions allow people to be efficient. If you take a closer look at quick decisions, are they really efficient all the time? Making assumptions about another person may often lead towards conflict. The number of legal claims within the business world shows evidence of its inefficiency (but also high profitability for the legal system). So when working with the Chinese, quick decisions can be deadly, since the basic values and beliefs are unique to their culture. If Chinese business leaders make what appears to be an illogical business decision, should you pass judgment on their decisions? Or have the right to do so?

For example, the label of child labor is one challenging topic. While it is common sense that we should not abuse children and place them into the workforce early in life, its practice in many developing countries may also be part of the lessons needed to develop in their journey. Many Western societies were able to learn those lessons in their development before and during the Industrial Revolution. The children of those times grew up to have a great appreciation for work and their accomplishments. Such an appreciation for hard work is one of the many struggles of developing nations currently. Perhaps, the experience of child labor is a necessary lesson for societies, to develop key morals and values from the experience.

Another challenging topic is the common one of bribery. While China faces this challenge at many local levels, the extent and determination of what is bribery is vague. Within Chinese culture, spending significant time with people on the personal side is a basic part of business. This requires many meals and relevant gifts that show respect and care. The development of relationships calls for certain gifts that are thoughtful and at times expensive. In the West, companies place monetary values on gifts but meals can be extravagant. Is there a consistency issue here with the amount of money spent in the West? How much money spent is bribery in one culture compared to another? Of course, there are clear limits to bribery when it comes to direct money exchanged. Bribery is definitely ethically challenging for many organizational leaders. How you define bribery based on one set of cultural values may not apply to other cultures. When looking at the issue, be conscious of other cultural values that drive behavior; refrain from blind judgment of others' behaviors alone.

The second characteristic of the contextual system is the practice of categorization. Within the practice of management, categorization is common. We tend to categorize people by their age, gender, profession, religious and ethnic backgrounds, physical appearance, etc. Once we place people into a category, certain characteristics place people into a box. This is another form of judgment. You may have a mental image of what a Chinese business leader may look like, or the characteristics of the Chinese. For example, many assume that Chinese workers are obedient. Such assumptions are dangerous as the Chinese people may not be that simple. We've discussed many differences based on region, age, and gender. With China going through such a massive transformation within two decades, many traditional characteristics simply do not apply. They can be anywhere in the continuum of traditional Chinese characteristics to Western ways of life.

The unconscious act of judgment will greatly limit your ability to be successful. The many novel behaviors and decisions you'll experience will most likely have very different logical rationales than what you see in your Western experiences. If you make simple judgments, lost are the vivid colors of the Chinese culture. Keeping an open mind and constantly seeking to understand will gain you the respect of the Chinese and help you be successful in any business venture.

Leadership within Hierarchy

What do you lose when ideas from subordinates are lost? Coming from many years of community rule, the Chinese have a clear sense of order. Their belief in a high power distance may often force people into conforming ways of work. Some may not openly share disagreements or ideas with their superiors. Yet, if we're looking to be competitive in a knowledge economy, we can't afford not to tap into the whole brain of the organization. Having conforming people in your organization will lead to stagnation, not to mention that it would be boring as well. From this perspective, let's make a distinction between leadership and management. While there are countless definitions of both in literature, management is concerned with tasks, projects, timelines, and efficiencies. It is a necessary part of business from a tangible perspective. Leadership, on the other hand, involves the people dimension. It seeks to inspire people and help them develop. The typical hierarchy in organizations and its corresponding conformist behaviors come from management. What happens if you inject leadership into the hierarchy?

Conventional thought tends to pit leadership and management on opposite sides of a battleground. Concepts such as turning the organizational pyramid upside down still traps people into a pyramid hierarchy. The question I tend to ask many executives is why are we stuck in that pyramid at all? Why do we have to live within a box (thinking outside the box) or a glass

(glass half full or half empty)? Why don't we eliminate the pyramid, box, and glass?

The exciting aspect of organizations and people is that they are both organic entities that have many dimensions of existence. Since we're competing in a global knowledge economy, does knowledge have to be within a hierarchy? While tasks and projects all have many dependencies that call for hierarchies, many other key dimensions of life don't exist in a hierarchy. For example, anyone can create knowledge that's valuable for businesses. At an emotional level (emotional intelligence), people's emotions do not exist on a hierarchy either. One person's emotions are not above or below another's emotions. Both knowledge and emotional intelligence are key aspects to a successful organization.

When working with the Chinese, knowledge represents the innovativeness of the people. Emotions represent the importance of relationships and the connections between people. Both of these do not have to be stuck within a formal hierarchy. As leaders entering a new market, allow knowledge and emotion to flow naturally. As managers, continue to navigate projects and efficiency but never forget the human factor. The Chinese have ample value in their innovativeness and relational orientation. Learn how to permeate the rigid boundaries of hierarchies in all organizations by identifying new dimensions that elevate your competitiveness.

Working Harder Is Not Enough

Is working hard enough for today's environment? One of the mental traps with many people is that time is linear and produces a linear outcome. During the industrial era, machines and labor produced the products. Like a car, stepping on the gas pedal gives you more speed. The linear dimension functioned well for those times. Unfortunately, we're no longer working in that era. Do the rules from those times still apply? Does the phrase "time is money" still apply?

Global companies today exist in a knowledge economy. Knowledge is not linear. People have "aha" moments at different times. The human brain can be exponentially efficient, if we know how to access that brilliance. Within this global economy, working hard will only get you so far. Working smarter is an ideal partner to success. For example, have you determined your hourly worth? Let's say you're worth $100/hour (just working with round numbers). Is it worth your time to be doing many activities such as checking endless amounts of email? Is it worth it for you to stand in line at the bank or the grocery store? If work-life balance is such a challenge, how might you think entrepreneurially about working smarter in all aspects of life? Rather than going shopping at "normal" times during the day, like after work when the stores are busy, why not go during non-busy times? You'll find it's much more efficient to have a closer parking space and no line at the cashier. How much time did you just make? With emails, how much time could you gain if you only saw your emails organized by priority and many repetitive questions disappear? Having a personal assistant for $15/hour gives you significant returns.

When working in China, these concepts become even more important. From a relationship perspective, you can work very hard to gain the needed relationships for business. Yet, you are constantly working uphill as a foreigner with only one lifetime's efforts. (Many of the Chinese people's relationships are generations old.) Learning to work smarter with relationships can leverage many existing relationships that are decades or even centuries old between families and friends. On one hand, you can spend a significant amount of time and money attempting to build many relationships (working hard). On the other, you can work smarter by establishing one or two key relationships that will obtain all the necessary relationships you'll need. We've discussed those strategic relationship ideas throughout the book.

Creating a New Paradigm of Education

How well can you learn new information? The concept of learning varies but still hinges on the human brain. From the Chinese education system, the primary focus is on achievement of a specific outcome. An examination-oriented system yields excellent learners as long as they are clear on the outcome. Within this paradigm, memorization and respect for authorities greatly limit creativity and decision-making skills. Furthermore, the learning process lacks a psychological understanding. Like the vocational movement of the 1900s, such a system creates great employees ready to follow instructions. Understanding the educational paradigm of the Chinese culture can leverage the strength of the culture's demand for further education without falling into the trap of creating obedient employees. Even more imperative, knowing your personal paradigm of learning is the context for long-term success.

Reflect on your paradigm of learning. How effective are you at learning new information? To be successful in China or in any other country, learning the endless amounts of cultural information and business norms is incredibly daunting. In concluding this book, I hope to provide you with a higher awareness to learning paradigms so that you'll be more effective. Focusing on the context of learning helps you create an open mind while maximizing your return on investment of time and money. To learn is to have a high level of retention on information gained. In order to retain information, receiving information is the first step.

There are three basic modalities of learning or communication: visual, kinesthetic, and auditory. In general, only 20 percent of the population is auditory learners. This is why we have phrases like "in one ear, out the other." Many people are simply not good at learning by listening alone. The other two modalities are an even split, approximately at 40 percent of the population. To receive information effectively, knowing how you learn and how others learn makes efficient use of time. You can find ample information on determining your modality by using the key search phrase "visual auditory kinesthetic learning styles" on the Web. Knowing your own modality can help you maximize efficiency in learning new information. If you are a kinesthetic learner, you learn most by taking action. Reading information or watching videos may not be enough. When you receive new information, apply it immediately so that retention is high. If you're a visual learner, take the time to ask for visual examples. The more you watch others in action, the more you'll retain the information. Using a preferred modality is very helpful for children as well. Most children are brilliant at learning; unfortunately, large classrooms don't allow educators to fully apply learning modalities. When students get bad grades, it may not be that they are not good students; in fact, they may still be brilliant learners. They simply did not receive the information in a modality they need. In many lecture-style classes, visual and kinesthetic learners may face various challenges. So as a leader in business, focus on using your context of learning to maximize retention. In a busy environment, time is scarce. You won't have too many opportunities to fail the recall of key cultural information in a business setting.

Modalities are also a powerful tool for building effective relationships. When engaging Chinese leaders, establishing the primary communication modality through basic conversations about personal topics is a wise strategic choice. The choice of words used by people is an indicator of their preferences. For example, when talking about a person's favorite weather, kinesthetic people may focus more on feelings such as being cold or hot. Visual people will focus more on the appearance such as sunny or cloudy. One response may resemble something like the following: "I love the warm weather. When the sun is out in the spring, I can go kayaking or hiking in the woods." An analysis of this statement indicates a high preference for a kinesthetic modality, since many action-oriented words are used. The word warmth indicates a physical sensation. The activities of kayaking and hiking both indicate physical activities. Visual is also the second preference in this example. Having the sun out in the spring is a visual clue. Both of the activities are outdoors, leading further towards a visual component of modalities. So as you engage in initial conversations with any Chinese leader, first take the time to analyze the words used to get a sense of their preferred communication modality. Once you understand people's learning modality, you save yourself a lot of time by communicating in their modality so that retention is high. In simple terms, the other person will see you as someone "similar" and an effective communicator. This is a foundation of a strong relationship.

Learning also requires significant application. Once you receive information in your preferred modality, retention happens when there's an emotional attachment. If a piece of information is important to you, make an effort to apply it and measure its results. For example, if you find out that a Chinese partner loves to play badminton, take the time to explore the sport by playing it or taking some lessons. Whether you like it or not is irrelevant. This allows you to have a strong connection to a favorite sport and share experiences. This is also how I've designed this book. While there's tremendous cultural information in the book, applying the information will significantly increase retention when you begin your journey in China. Many of the activities help to solidify the concepts so that when you experience China, you'll be able to easily recall the information in the book and apply the skills you've developed. Learning is a key skill when entering any new environment.

I'll leave you with a few reflective questions to ponder as you begin your journey:

- How am I keeping an open mind towards the Chinese ways of business conduct?
- How can I refrain from applying Western rules of life towards the Chinese people? (Refrain from judgment.)
- What kind of leader do I wish to be in an international business venture, and how do I live up to it everyday?

Reflect on these often, perhaps once a week, taking different questions at a time. Journal your thoughts to visualize your journey. Doing business overseas can be a life-altering experience for many people. Making a conscious choice to learn and grow from it without blame or judgment is a key competence of a successful business leader. I wish you the best of luck in your journey as learners and business leaders.

RECOMMENDED READING

* Books on my top eight nonfiction list that have made a profound impact on my journey.

GENERAL PERSPECTIVES

Ellis, Yi S. and Bryan D. Ellis. *101 Stories for Foreigners to Understand Chinese People.* Shenyang, China: Liaoning Education Press, 2007.

Fannin, Rebecca. *Silicon Dragon: How China Is Winning the Tech Race.* New York: McGraw-Hill 2007.

Wang, Mengkui. *China's Economy.* Translated by Bingwen Lui. Beijing, China: China International Press, 2004.

Zinzius, Birgit. *Doing Business in the New China: A Handbook and Guide.* Westport, CT: Praeger, 2004.

LEADERSHIP PERSPECTIVES

Baker, Dave, Cathy Greenberg, and Collins Hemingway. *What Happy Companies Know: How The New Science Of Happiness Can Change Your Company For The Better.* Upper Saddle River, NJ: Pearson Prentice Hall, 2006.

Bass, Bernard M. *Bass & Stogdill's Handbook of Leadership.* 3rd ed. New York: Free Press, 1990.

Checkland, Peter. *Systems Thinking, Systems Practice: A 30 Year Retrospective.* New York: John Wiley & Sons, Inc., 1999.

* Clawson, James G. *Level Three Leadership: Getting Below the Surface.* 3rd ed. New York: Pearson, 2006.

Collins, Jim C. *Good to Great: Why Some Companies Make The Leap . . . And Others Don't.* New York: Harper Collins, 2001.

DeFrank, Richard S., and John M. Ivancevich, "Stress on the Job: An Executive Update," *Academy of Management Executive* 12(3) (1998): 55–66.

Drucker, Peter F. *Post-Capitalist Society.* Oxford: Butterworth Heonemann, 1993.

Ghoshal, Sumantra, "Bad Management Theories Are Destroying Good Management Practices," *Academy of Management Learning & Education* 4(1) (March 2005): 75–91.

* Jacques, Roy. *Manufacturing The Employee: Management Knowledge from the 19th to 21st Centuries.* Thousand Oaks, CA: Sage Publications, 1996.

Kotter, John P. *Leading Change.* Boston, MA: Harvard Business School Press, 1996.

Lumpkin, Gregory T., and Gregory G. Dess. "Clarifying the Entrepreneurial Orientation Construct and Linking It to Performance." *Academy of Management Review* 21 (1996): 135–73.

Paul, Richard, and Linda Elder. "Critical Thinking: The Art of Socratic Questioning" *Journal of Developmental Education* 31(1) (Fall 2007): 36–7.

Reinhard, Tess. "A Grounded Theory Investigation of Change Leadership During Turbulent Times."PhD diss., Northern Illinois University, 2000. ProQuest Dissertations & Theses: Full Text database. (UMI No. 3272165).

Robbins, Stephen P. *Essentials of Organizational Behavior.* Upper Saddle River, NJ: Prentice Hall, 2005.

Schein, Edgar H. *The Corporate Culture Survival Guide.* San Francisco, CA: Jossey-Bass, 1999.

———. *Organizational Culture and Leadership.* San Francisco, CA: Jossey-Bass, 1992.

Senge, Peter M. *The Fifth Discipline: The Age and Practice of The Learning Organization.* London: Century Business, 1990.

Sun, Ted. "Business as an Agent of World Benefit: Management Knowledge Leading Positive Change." Paper presented at the United Nations Global Forum: Business as an Agent of World Benefit: Management Knowledge Leading Positive Change, Case Western Reserve University, January 4, 2007.

———. *Survival Tactics: Top 11 Behaviors of Successful Entrepreneurs.* Westport, CT: Greenwood Publishing Group, 2007.

Tucker, Aaron A. "Leadership by the Socratic Method." *Air & Space Power Journal* 21(2) (Summer 2007): 80–7.

Williams, Lloyd C. *The Congruence of People and Organizations: Healing Dysfunction from the Inside Out.* Westport, CT: Quorum Books, 1993.

———. *Creating the Congruence Workplace: Challenges for People and Their Organizations.* Westport, CT: Quorum Books, 2002.

PSYCHOLOGY & PHILOSOPHICAL PERSPECTIVES

* Bavister, Steve, and Amanda Vickers. *Teach Yourself NLP.* Chicago: Contemporary Books, 2004.

* Cooper, Robert K., and Ayman Sawaf. *Executive EQ: Emotional Intelligence in Business.* Berkeley, CA: Berkley Publishing Group, 1998.

* Gardner, Howard. *Multiple Intelligences: The Theory In Practice.* New York: Basic Books, 1993.

Gazzaniga, Michael S. *The Mind's Past.* Berkeley, CA: University of California Press, 1998.

* Jung, Carl. G. *The Undiscovered Self.* New York: Penguin Group, Inc., 1958.

Krell, David Farrell, ed. *Martin Heidegger Basic Writings: From Being and Time (1927) to The Task of Thinking (1964)*. New York: HarperCollins, 1993.

Landy, Frank L., and Jeffrey M. Conte. *Work in the 21st Century: An Introduction to Industrial and Organizational Psychology*. New York: McGraw Hill Companies, 2004.

Moser, Paul K., and Arnold vander Nat. *Human Knowledge: Classical and Contemporary Approaches* New York: Oxford University Press, 1995.

* Ormrod, Jeanne E. *Educational Psychology: Developing Learners*. Upper Saddle River, NJ: Pearson, 2006.

Rokeach, Milton. *The Nature Of Human Values*. New York: Free Press, 1973.

Smith, Malcolm K. "Malcolm Knowles, Informal Adult Education, Self-direction and Andragogy," the encyclopedia of informal education, www.infed.org/thinkers/et-knowl.htm.

Sternberg, Robert J. *Cognitive Psychology*, 4th ed. Belmont, CA: Thomson Wadsworth, 2006.

CULTURAL PERSPECTIVES

Aycan, Zeynep, Rabindra N. Kanungo, Manuel Mendonca, Kaicheng Yu, Jurgen Deller, Gunter Stahl, and Anwar Kurshid. "Impact of Culture on Human Resource Management Practices: A 10-Country Comparison." *Applied Psychology: An International Review* 49(1) (January 2000): 192.

Bo, Jin. *Understanding China: Introduction to China's History, Society and Culture*. Beijing, China: China Intercontinental Press, 2008.

Chen, Ming-Jer. *Inside Chinese Business: A Guide for Managers Worldwide*. Boston: Harvard Business Press, 2001.

Hay Group. "East Meets West: Bridging Two Great Business Cultures, March 2007." http://content.ll-0.com/haygroup1/east.pdf?i=062707122034 (accessed November 13, 2008).

* Hofstede, Geert. *Culture's Consequences: Comparing Values, Behaviors, Institutions, and Organizations across Nations*, 2nd ed. Thousand Oaks: Sage Publications, 2000.

Seligman, Scott D. *Chinese Business Etiquette: A Guide to Protocol, Manners and Cultures in the People's Republic of China*. New York: Warner Books Inc., 1999.

Wei, Ran, and Zhongdang Pan. "Mass media and consumerist values in the People's Republic of China." *International Journal of Public Opinion Research* 11 (1999): 75–96.

MANAGEMENT PERSPECTIVES

Development Dimensions International, Inc., "Employee Retention in China 2007: The Flight of Human Talent." *China Business Review* (July-August 2008).

Farrell, Diana, and Andrew J. Grant. "China's Looming Talent Shortage: The Emerging Global Labor Market." *McKinley Quarterly* (*The Online Journal of McKinley & Co.*), no. 4 (2005) http://www.dryvonnesum.com/pdf/China_Looming_Talent_Shortage_McKinsey_Qtrly_Oct_2005.pdf accessed March 15, 2009).

Leung, Thomas, and L. L. Yeung. "Negotiation in the People's Republic of China: Results of a Survey of Small Business in Hong Kong," *Journal of Small Business Management* 33, no. I (1995): 73.

Ma, Shaozhuang, and Virginia Trigo, "Winning the War for Managerial Talent in China: An Empirical Study." *Chinese Economy*, 41(3) (May 2008): 34–57.

MARKETING PERSPECTIVES

Ahmed, Sadrudin, and Alain d'Astous. *Consumer Behavior in Asia: Issues and Marketing Practice.* New York: Haworth Press, 1999.

Cui, Geng. "Segmenting China's Consumer Market: A Hybrid Approach." *Journal of International Consumer Marketing* 11 (1999): 55–76.

Cui, G., and Q. Liu. "Regional Market Segments of China: Opportunities and Barriers in a Big Emerging Market." *Journal of Consumer Marketing* 17 (2000): 55–72.

Dickson, Marsha A., Sharron J. Lennon, Catherine P. Montalto, Dong Shen, and Li Zhang. "Chinese Consumer Market Segments for Foreign Apparel." *Journal of Consumer Marketing* 21 (2004): 301–317.

Emerald Group Publishing Limited, "Selling to China's Rich and Not So Rich: Need to Go beyond the Luxury Market". *Strategic Direction* 21 (2005): 5–7.

Fischer, Thomas, Heiko Gebauer, and Elgar Fleisch. "Redefining Product Strategies in China: Overcoming Barriers to Enter the Medium Market Segment." *Strategic Direction* 24 (2008): 3–5.

Sum, Siu Wai, and Liu Zhi Chao, "Marketing in Chinese Small and Medium Enterprises (SMEs): The State of the Art in a Chinese Socialist Economy." *Small Business Economics* 25 (2005): 333–46.

Tse, Alan C.B., Leo Y.M. Sin, Oliver H.M. Yau, Jenny S.Y. Lee, and Raymond Chow. "A Firm's Role in the Marketplace and the Relative Importance of Market Orientation and Relationship Marketing Orientation." *European Journal of Marketing* 38 (2004), 1158–72.

Zhang, Zhiming, Yi Li, Chen Gong, and Haidong Wu. "Casual Wear Product Attributes: A Chinese Consumers' Perspective." *Journal of Fashion Marketing and Management* 6 (2002): 53–62.

Ethical and Legal Perspectives

Blackburn, John D., Elliot I. Klayman, and Martin H. Malin. *The Legal Environment Of Business*. Boston Irwin, 1994.

Cheng, Li-ru, and Xuan Zhou. "Characteristic of the New Policy System of Chinese Foreign Direct Investment," *China-USA Business Review* 6(3) (March 2007): 19–22.

Ciulla, Joanne B. *The Ethics of Leadership*. Belmont, CA: Thomson Wadsworth, 2003.

Harshman, Carl, and Ellen Harshman. "The Gordian Knot of Ethics: Understanding Leadership Effectiveness and Ethical Behavior." *Journal of Business Ethics* 78(1/2) (March 2008): 175–92.

Needham High School's World History Web Site. "Child Labor in Factories: A New Workforce during the Industrial Revolution." Needham High School, http://nhs.needham.k12.ma.us/cur/Baker_00/2002_p7/ak_p7/childlabor.html (accessed March 15, 2009).

Tian, Qing. "Perception of Business Bribery in China: The Impact of Moral Philosophy." *Journal of Business Ethics* 80, no. 3 (July 2008): 437–45.

APPENDIX

This is the survey instrument sent to both Chinese and Western businesspeople. The results are in part the basis for the conclusions reached in this book.

Values-Beliefs Survey

Dear Participants,

Thank you very much for taking part in this historical study concerning values and beliefs that drive human behavior and decisions. Within the context of a global economy, reaching out to someone on the other side of the world is relatively simple. Moving beyond conventional thinking often demands exploration of corresponding behaviors within specific countries that often display a very limited understanding of the underpinning challenges embedded in thought and action. In order to grasp the core foundations of any culture (and its generational and regional uniqueness), this study will seek to understand the core values and beliefs of your people and asks you to partner with me, the researcher in more accurately determining the essential values that define and describe YOU. As you hold an in-depth knowledge of your people, your challenges and perspectives on economic development in your country, your understanding of the challenges and opportunities that ensure regional stability and your potential for earnings increase in a global economy. Please respond honestly to the statements in this survey. You may find that the instrument is a <u>development tool</u> that allows YOU to further understand self as well.

The information you provide will be analyzed from a global perspective in comparison with other nations and the results shall be in aggregate form to ensure your confidentiality. As such, it is hopeful that the anonymity and confidentiality increases your willingness to truthfully engage the questions in the surveys. Future workshops and books will also accompany the research findings, with your expressed written permission, so that your organization AND you can achieve massive international business success without having to memorize countless behaviors.

> *Sincerely,*
> *Dr. Ted Sun*
> *Chief Dream Maker*
> *Author of* Survival Tactics *(2007) & the coming book:*
> Inside the Chinese Business Mind *(expected 2010)*

1. Your Age:

2. Gender: Male _____ Female _____

3. Please identify your position in the business:

_____ President/CEO
_____ Executive Management
_____ Management
_____ Technical/Professional
_____ Non-technical/Office staff
_____ Manual Labor

4. Country of Residence:

United States
China
United Kingdom
France
Switzerland
Germany
Austria

5. Region/State of Residence:

6. Type of Organization:

_____ Government
_____ State/government owned Enterprise
_____ Private For Profit Business
_____ Non-profit organization
_____ Multinational Organization

7. Indicate your level of formal education:

_____ High School graduate
_____ Vocational College graduate
_____ University graduate
_____ Graduate/professional degree
_____ Doctoral / PhD

8. Primary Educational Background (mark the item most appropriate)

_____ Science, engineering or technical
_____ Social Science or Humanities
_____ Business
_____ Professional (law, health field, social services)
_____ Other educational background (please add)

Step 1. Please select the **top 8 values** that are most important to you from the following list. Please establish a priority listing for the 8 values in order of priority with 1 being the most important to you.

Personal Achievement/ Excellence	Courage	Freedom	Legacy	Security
Organizational Achievement/ Excellence	Decisiveness	Friendship	Loyalty	Service/Helpful
Adventure/ Challenge	Democracy	Fun/Happiness	Order	Simplicity
Authority	Dependability	Growth	Optimism	Speed/Fast Pace
Balance	Diversity	Honesty	Passion	Spirituality
Career	Ecological Awareness	Independence	Perfection	Stability
Change	Efficiency	Influence	Pride	Status
Comfort	Empathy/Kind	Inner Harmony	Privacy	Structure
Community	Fairness	Innovation/ Creativity	Quality	Teamwork
Competence	Fame	Integrity	Recognition	Trust
Competition	Family	Intensity	Religion (this should not only refer to religion but also something like belief)	Wisdom
Cooperation	Financial Independence	Knowledge	Respect	
Country	Health	Leadership	Responsibility	

Step 2. Please respond to the following statements.

The following questions are designed to gain an understanding of your thoughts regarding your values and beliefs. **The *"degree of importance scale"* is designed to determine how *important the statement* is to you.** The following key applies to the "Degree of Importance Scale":

1. – Very unimportant
2. – Unimportant
3. – Slightly unimportant
4. – Slightly important
5. – Important
6. – Very important

The "Behavior Alignment" is designed to seek your actual behavior in accordance with the statement. Please be as honest as possible. The following key applies to the "Behavior Alignment Scale":

1. – Strongly disagree
2. – Disagree
3. – Slightly disagree
4. – Slight agree
5. – Agree
6. – Strongly agree

1. Personal Achievement/ Excellence	I have great ambitions for myself. I expect the highest levels of excellence for my work. My work does not have to be the best. I am very ambitious with my goals. I am aggressive when it comes to my goals.
2. Organizational Achievement/ Excellence	My organization will have great achievements. My organization always works to the highest levels of excellence. Organizational excellence defines my success.
3. Adventure/Challenge	I enjoy taking on new tasks. I thrive being challenged by other people. I proactively take on risks that help me learn.
4. Authority	I follow the directions given by my supervisor. I often challenge the decisions passed down from management. I do not question my superior's decisions.
5. Balance	I have a high focus on work/life balance. Life balance is my definition of success. I make sure to have leisure time in the midst of busy work schedules.
6. Career	My career is my top priority for success. Advancement opportunities drive me to work harder. I have high expectations for my career.
7. Change	I am comfortable with changes in the workplace. Change makes me uncomfortable. I actively create change around me.
8. Comfort	I want my life to be relaxed. I tend to avoid pressure in the workplace. Comfort is a high priority for me.
9. Community	I want my work to contribute to society as a whole. My achievements are only important for me. I feel a sense of responsibility to my community.

10. Competence	A mastery of skills enhances my career. My advancement requires a high level of expertise. Skills in my job are more important than my social network.
11. Competition	I have to compete with others in order to advance. Competition is what makes me better. I have a passion for winning.
12. Cooperation	I always seek to work well with others. Reaching an agreement is crucial to relationships, even if I do not personally agree. I enjoy working alone.
13. Country	Helping my country should be part of my work. I have a patriotic nature. I am proud to be a citizen of my country.
14. Courage	I enjoy being outside of my comfort zone. I actively seek uncomfortable situations to grow. I have a strong will to do what I feel is right.
15. Decisiveness	I am quick to make decisions. I do not make decisions until I have all of the information. My decisions are well thought out.
16. Democracy	Everyone should be involved when making decisions. Sharing power with the group makes sense. Collective decisions are ideal in the workplace. People in authority should make the tough decisions.
17. Dependability	People can depend on me. My friends often count on me for help. I am usually the last to respond when a friend calls for help.
18. Diversity	I am conscious of the uniqueness of other people. People from different cultures have value in the workplace. I enjoy working with people who are different.
19. Ecological awareness	Environmental concerns are always on my mind. I am appreciative of the environment. Working for a green company is my dream.
20. Efficiency	I focus significant amount of energy on getting faster at tasks. Working smarter is my way to success. Working less to achieve the same outcome is one of my common practices.
21. Empathy/Kind	I am always kind to people.

(Continued)

(Continued)

	Being sincere to others is a way of life for me. I have a lot of compassion for others. I often forgive others.
22. Fairness	All people deserve to have their equal share. I often step aside so that others can have their chance. The wealth of a few individuals should be shared equally in my community.
23. Fame	I enjoy being the center of attention. If I had a chance, I would want to be on TV. People should see the work that I do.
24. Family	I spend significant time with family. I enjoy being close to significant others. Every aspect about work is for my family. My family is the purpose of my achievements. My hard work is to make my family proud.
25. Financial Independence	I have steady income to meet my needs. My desires for material objects are satisfied with sufficient income. Making money is my road to independence.
26. Health	Emotional health is just as important as physical health. I strive for physical fitness with daily exercise. I actively communicate my emotions. I eat well to maintain my health.
27. Freedom (#5 from China class)	I rarely have the time to do what I want. My responsibilities control my schedule. I have ample time to choose activities freely. I have the right to choose my path.
28. Friendship	My friends and I are very close. I share my thoughts and dreams with friends. I need to have friends who understand me.
29. Fun/Happiness	I desire lots of excitement in my life. Laughing often is part of my life. I am as happy as I was in my younger years.
30. Growth	I constantly seek professional development. Ongoing learning gives me the needed intellectual stimulation. There are always advancement opportunities in my life.

31. Honesty	I always speak the truth 100% at all times. People's feelings are more important than the entire truth. I will tell the truth up to a point where respect is concerned. I will tell the truth up to the point where I perceive feelings will be hurt.
32. Independence	I need to have control over my own schedule. My supervisor should give me complete autonomy in my work. I can work without much supervision.
33. Influence	I am able to shift people's decisions on various matters. Swaying the thoughts of other people gets me what I want. I like to include others to obtain mutual agreement on issues.
34. Inner Harmony	My daily actions align with my values. Inner peace comes from my moral fulfillment. Being ethical gives me a peace of mind.
35. Innovation/Creativity	I like being on the cutting edge of technology. Solving problems in different ways keeps me interested in my work. My imagination contributes greatly to my work.
36. Integrity	I always follow through with my promises. A person's word defines the individual. No matter the consequence, I always stand up for my beliefs.
37. Intensity	I enjoy working in a high-pressure environment. High-pressure workplace gets the best out of me. I don't like to be pressured.
38. Knowledge	I surround myself with experts in my field to learn from them. I seek to gain expert power. I have a constant thirst for new information.
39. Leadership	Positional power is the way to reach the top. My presence often energizes people. I take charge of projects.
40. Legacy	I am conscious of how people will remember me. Individual achievement does not matter. In the long run, no one will remember what I have accomplished.

(*Continued*)

(Continued)

41. Loyalty	I am committed to the goals of my team.
	I am faithful to my organization.
	I have stuck with my organization for many years.
42. Order	Being in control creates order in my world.
	I have to sacrifice my individuality to follows rules.
	I always obey the laws.
	Rules are essential for me to live with others.
43. Optimism (#5 from China class)	I see a positive journey ahead of me.
	I look forward to each day's adventures.
	I feel hopeful of a brighter future.
44. Passion	I am aware of what I enjoy the most in life.
	My work involves high emotional engagement.
	I get into heated debates with people at work.
45. Perfection	I need to do something very well before letting it go.
	I am always reaching to be the best.
	I have a low tolerance for error.
46. Pride	I take enormous pride in my actions.
	I keep my head high at all times.
	I care about the work that I do.
47. Privacy	People should not know everything about me.
	The government should keep its eyes out of my world.
	I keep many secrets from others.
48. Quality	Excellence of outcomes defines my work.
	The speed of completion of the project is not as important as the outcome.
	Doing it well should be everyone's goal.
49. Recognition	I like to be recognized publicly for my work.
	I am a role model for others often.
	I should get credit for my work at all times.
50. Religion	I attend church/temple every week.
	The religious texts offer many solutions to my problems.
	Life guidance comes from the church/temple.
51. Respect	I will only work for a company that pays me a fair wage for my efforts.
	I treat others as they want to be treated.
	People should be treated equally.
52. Responsibility	I am accountable for my actions.
	If something I did goes wrong in my project, I will always have a role in that failure.

	When a project I am involved in fails, someone else screwed up. I am responsible for my own success in life.
53. Security	I need assurance for my job. I am always concerned with having enough food. Plenty of jobs exist for me.
54. Service/Helpful	Helping others give me great satisfaction. When people ask me for help, I can't turn them down. I like to improve other people's circumstances.
55. Simplicity	A busy schedule gives me headaches. I want to live with minimal complexity. I like having a busy schedule.
56. Speed/Fast Pace	I like having pressure to work fast. Aggressive deadlines bring out the best in me. I like to take my time when working.
57. Spirituality	I have a sense of my purpose. Life is about a higher calling within my soul. I have an individual connection to a higher power.
58. Stability	I want a predictable life. Daily routines minimize my stress levels. I like having each day be different.
59. Status	Being higher on a hierarchy gives me respect. I like being recognized as someone important. I need to drive a better car to show my achievements.
60. Structure	I plan my days carefully. I prefer to work in an environment that changes little. Formal process helps people live organized lives.
61. Teamwork	I enjoy working with people toward a common goal. Collaboration with teammates yields great achievements. I like to work closely with others.
62. Trust	My most powerful relationship has a foundation of mutual trust. I always do what I say. Making money is more important than following through with my commitments.
63. Wisdom	Having knowledge is not enough for me to be successful. I need to have a clear understanding of myself. I am able to see the system of people as a whole.

(*Continued*)

Degree of Importance Scale	Statement	Behavior Alignment Scale
1. . .2. . .3. . .4. . .5. . .6	A clear hierarchy provides a clear goal for me.	1. . .2. . .3. . .4. . .5. . .6
1. . .2. . .3. . .4. . .5. . .6	Employees should conform to decisions made by executives.	1. . .2. . .3. . .4. . .5. . .6
1. . .2. . .3. . .4. . .5. . .6	Employees should have input on decisions that impact them.	1. . .2. . .3. . .4. . .5. . .6
1. . .2. . .3. . .4. . .5. . .6	Foreigners are just like us.	1. . .2. . .3. . .4. . .5. . .6
1. . .2. . .3. . .4. . .5. . .6	Having a clear hierarchy is good for our society.	1. . .2. . .3. . .4. . .5. . .6
1. . .2. . .3. . .4. . .5. . .6	Having a great working relationship with my manager is more important than a given task.	1. . .2. . .3. . .4. . .5. . .6
1. . .2. . .3. . .4. . .5. . .6	I always find ways to resolve problems.	1. . .2. . .3. . .4. . .5. . .6
1. . .2. . .3. . .4. . .5. . .6	I am able to always achieve the goals that are important to me.	1. . .2. . .3. . .4. . .5. . .6
1. . .2. . .3. . .4. . .5. . .6	I am aware of what is important.	1. . .2. . .3. . .4. . .5. . .6
1. . .2. . .3. . .4. . .5. . .6	I based my decisions on my economics.	1. . .2. . .3. . .4. . .5. . .6
1. . .2. . .3. . .4. . .5. . .6	I can remember many times how I was able to get out of trouble.	1. . .2. . .3. . .4. . .5. . .6
1. . .2. . .3. . .4. . .5. . .6	I consider myself successful in my life.	1. . .2. . .3. . .4. . .5. . .6
1. . .2. . .3. . .4. . .5. . .6	I do not need my company's leaders to take care of me.	1. . .2. . .3. . .4. . .5. . .6
1. . .2. . .3. . .4. . .5. . .6	I do not spend my time worrying about tomorrow.	1. . .2. . .3. . .4. . .5. . .6
1. . .2. . .3. . .4. . .5. . .6	I enjoy complete independence over my life.	1. . .2. . .3. . .4. . .5. . .6

1. . .2. . .3. . .4. . .5. . .6	I enjoy completing tasks my own way, rather than being told how to do it.	1. . .2. . .3. . .4. . .5. . .6
1. . .2. . .3. . .4. . .5. . .6	I feel satisfied with owning my career.	1. . .2. . .3. . .4. . .5. . .6
1. . .2. . .3. . .4. . .5. . .6	I have achieved my own personal happiness.	1. . .2. . .3. . .4. . .5. . .6
1. . .2. . .3. . .4. . .5. . .6	I have ample money.	1. . .2. . .3. . .4. . .5. . .6
1. . .2. . .3. . .4. . .5. . .6	I have no control over events in my life.	1. . .2. . .3. . .4. . .5. . .6
1. . .2. . .3. . .4. . .5. . .6	I have no idea why I am alive.	1. . .2. . .3. . .4. . .5. . .6
1. . .2. . .3. . .4. . .5. . .6	I need someone to tell me what to do with details.	1. . .2. . .3. . .4. . .5. . .6
1. . .2. . .3. . .4. . .5. . .6	I receive personal gratification working in my field.	1. . .2. . .3. . .4. . .5. . .6
1. . .2. . .3. . .4. . .5. . .6	I sacrifice my needs at work to maintain positive relationships.	1. . .2. . .3. . .4. . .5. . .6
1. . .2. . .3. . .4. . .5. . .6	I should be given room to complete tasks as I see fit.	1. . .2. . .3. . .4. . .5. . .6
1. . .2. . .3. . .4. . .5. . .6	I understand my purpose in life.	1. . .2. . .3. . .4. . .5. . .6
1. . .2. . .3. . .4. . .5. . .6	I want to be in charge.	1. . .2. . .3. . .4. . .5. . .6
1. . .2. . .3. . .4. . .5. . .6	I will sacrifice my personal desires for those of the community.	1. . .2. . .3. . .4. . .5. . .6
1. . .2. . .3. . .4. . .5. . .6	In difficult situations, I am capable of finding a way out.	1. . .2. . .3. . .4. . .5. . .6
1. . .2. . .3. . .4. . .5. . .6	Individual wealth is the building block of our society.	1. . .2. . .3. . .4. . .5. . .6
1. . .2. . .3. . .4. . .5. . .6	Leaders in my company should take care of subordinates.	1. . .2. . .3. . .4. . .5. . .6

(Continued)

(*Continued*)

1. . .2. . .3. . .4. . .5. . .6	Management must control their people to create products/services.	1. . .2. . .3. . .4. . .5. . .6
1. . .2. . .3. . .4. . .5. . .6	My company should take care of my needs.	1. . .2. . .3. . .4. . .5. . .6
1. . .2. . .3. . .4. . .5. . .6	My life is meaningful.	1. . .2. . .3. . .4. . .5. . .6
1. . .2. . .3. . .4. . .5. . .6	My organization's revenue growth is a prime objective for success.	1. . .2. . .3. . .4. . .5. . .6
1. . .2. . .3. . .4. . .5. . .6	My personal growth comes before organizational needs.	1. . .2. . .3. . .4. . .5. . .6
1. . .2. . .3. . .4. . .5. . .6	My personal time is more important than work needs.	1. . .2. . .3. . .4. . .5. . .6
1. . .2. . .3. . .4. . .5. . .6	Negative events happen to me all the time.	1. . .2. . .3. . .4. . .5. . .6
1. . .2. . .3. . .4. . .5. . .6	Our community success determines my success.	1. . .2. . .3. . .4. . .5. . .6
1. . .2. . .3. . .4. . .5. . .6	People from other countries cannot be trusted.	1. . .2. . .3. . .4. . .5. . .6
1. . .2. . .3. . .4. . .5. . .6	People in general are trustworthy.	1. . .2. . .3. . .4. . .5. . .6
1. . .2. . .3. . .4. . .5. . .6	Relationship is more important than winning.	1. . .2. . .3. . .4. . .5. . .6
1. . .2. . .3. . .4. . .5. . .6	Respect is more important than money.	1. . .2. . .3. . .4. . .5. . .6
1. . .2. . .3. . .4. . .5. . .6	The community guides my actions.	1. . .2. . .3. . .4. . .5. . .6
1. . .2. . .3. . .4. . .5. . .6	The community's goals for advancement are my top priority.	1. . .2. . .3. . .4. . .5. . .6
1. . .2. . .3. . .4. . .5. . .6	The needs of my community come before my personal needs.	1. . .2. . .3. . .4. . .5. . .6
1. . .2. . .3. . .4. . .5. . .6	We should not accept high degrees of inequality in our society.	1. . .2. . .3. . .4. . .5. . .6

Please add any comments that have emerged for you during the completion of this survey instrument.

Since you've placed some work into this assessment, feel free to see if people who are important to you can guess your top values as you've stated. This will be a fun exploration conversation for you and could lead to further understanding—which builds solid relationships.

THANK YOU SO VERY MUCH FOR YOUR WILLINGNESS TO PARTICIPATE IN THIS RESEARCH STUDY

Dr. Ted Sun, Chief Dream Maker

INDEX

ABOUT THE AUTHOR

Dr. Ted Sun is President and CEO of Executive Balance, an executive development and consulting firm for passionate organizations. Dr. Sun has taught many leaders transformational principles that have reshaped their lives. Major leaders around the world have learned to break traditional boundaries through systemic thought developed in their engagements with Dr. Sun. They include government leaders to executives of various global organizations. Dr. Sun also leads curriculum development and global residency programs, in over 32 countries, in the School of Business at SMC University, along with other leadership roles such as adjunct professor, course designer, and/or faculty developer at a number of other universities including City University, Southern New Hampshire University, and South University. At SMC University, Dr. Sun developed some of the most innovative business programs in the world, synthesizing systems thinking and emotional intelligence within the curriculum. His work on an international level is spread across many continents including Europe, Asia, and Africa. He presented his latest research on global business topics such as the critical need to shift from change management to change leadership, at the fall 2009 conference in Istanbul, Turkey with the International Academy of Management and Business. He is the author of *Survival Tactics: The Top 11 Behaviors of Successful Entrepreneurs* (Praeger, 2007).